The
Turtle

An Owner's Guide To

A HAPPY HEALTHY PET

Howell Book House

Howell Book House
A Simon & Schuster Macmillan Company
1633 Broadway
New York, NY 10019

Library of Congress Cataloging-in-Publication Data
Flank, Lenny.
The turtle : an owner's guide to a happy, healthy pet /Lenny Flank
p. cm.
ISBN: 0-87605-499-8

1. Turtles as pets. I. Title.
SF459.T8F53   1996
639.3'92—dc20   96-46119
                          CIP

Manufactured in the United States of America
10 9 8 7 6 5 4 3 2 1

Series Director: Ariel Cannon
Series Assistant Director: Jennifer Liberts
Book Design: Michele Laseau
Cover Design: Iris Jeromnimon
Illustration: Marvin Van Tiem III
Photography:
  Front cover and inset: Bill Love, back cover: Jean Wentworth
  Bill Love: 5, 7, 12, 18, 21, 22, 23, 27, 31, 32, 33, 35, 73, 76, 78, 99, 102, 103, 104, 107, 108, 109, 110, 111, 112, 113, 114
  Renee Stockdale: 6, 11, 13, 24–25, 29, 37, 40, 46, 48, 49, 50, 51, 56, 59, 62, 64, 65, 70, 71, 72, 77, 82, 85, 86, 87, 88–89, 92, 97, 101, 115
  Scott McKiernan: 8
  Joan Balzarini: 9, 26, 28, 30, 74, 75, 87, 100, 106
  Factor: 20
  Jean Wentworth: 94
Production Team: Kathleen Caulfield, Holly Wittenberg, Terri Sheehan, Angel Perez, David Faust, Natalie Hollifield, Stephanie Mohler and John Carroll

Contents

part one

Welcome to the World of the Turtle

part two

Living with Turtles

part three

Turtles in Our World

part four

Beyond the Basics

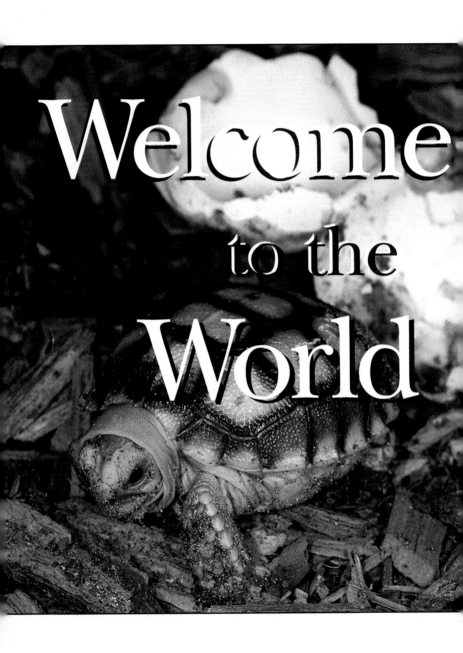

Welcome to the World

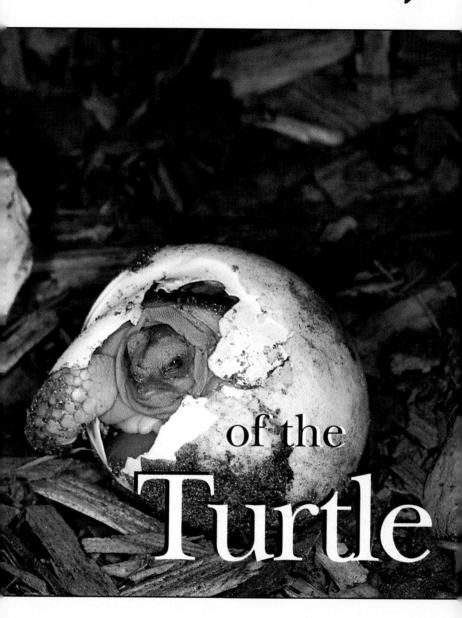

of the
Turtle

External Features of the Turtle

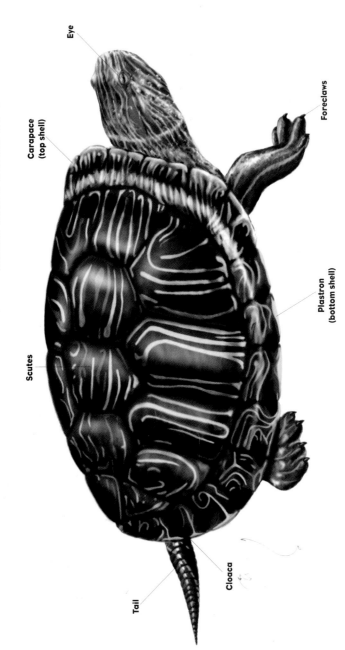

Carapace
(top shell)

Eye

Foreclaws

Scutes

Plastron
(bottom shell)

Cloaca

Tail

chapter 1

What
Is a
Turtle?

There is perhaps no more easily recognizable animal on earth than a turtle. While there are lizards that look like snakes, and salamanders that look like lizards, no other living creature looks remotely like a turtle. With their calm dispositions and brightly colored shells, turtles have been spared the enmity with which most other reptiles are usually regarded. Unlike lizards and snakes, which are

almost universally reviled, turtles are usually regarded as charming and attractive creatures. Few people, even the most intense reptile haters, are afraid of turtles.

A few decades ago, every five-and-dime store in the country was stuffed with tiny, bright-green baby turtles, usually found in a shallow water tray complete with a tiny plastic island and palm tree. Unfortunately, few of the many thousands of people who purchased these little creatures had any real idea how to care for them, and most of them ended up in a watery grave after a few months. This dreadful mortality rate, combined with some exaggerated fears about the spread of disease by turtles, virtually put an end to the turtle pet trade.

Today, however, we have become more knowledgeable about the natural world and the role that is played in it by various animals—including reptiles—and turtles have once again become popular as pets.

This Eastern box turtle enjoys having his neck tickled by his companion.

This book was written as a guide for the beginning turtle keeper, allowing new hobbyists to keep their pets happy and healthy. Although keeping turtles and tortoises in captivity is not difficult, there are a few potential problems that turtle keepers must be aware of, and a few rules and procedures that must be followed if these animals are to thrive in captivity. Our knowledge of how to meet the needs of captive reptiles has expanded enormously in just the past few years, and even though this book is aimed primarily at beginners, I hope that it can serve as a useful reference for more experienced turtle keepers as well.

Biology of Turtles & Tortoises

There are about 220 species of turtles living today, less than one-tenth the number of living snakes or lizards. Despite their relative lack of diversity, however, turtles are hardy and adaptable animals, and have moved into a wide variety of habitats, from hot arid deserts to the open seas. In size, they range from the tiny Musk turtle, less than five inches long, to the huge marine Leatherback, which reaches lengths of

These two African Spurred tortoises hatched from their eggs just minutes before this photo was taken.

over six feet and weighs more than half a ton. The largest living land turtle, the Galapagos tortoise, can reach a length of four and a half feet and weigh over 550 pounds.

All turtles are reptiles, a class of animals charac- terized by dry scaly skin, a dependence upon external heat sources rather than internal metabolism and a shelled egg that can be laid on land.

"ECTOTHERMIC" ANIMALS

Like all other reptiles and amphibians, turtles are "ectothermic," meaning they cannot produce their own internal body heat. Such a system of metabolism is sometimes referred to as being "cold-blooded," but this is not a very accurate term, since some desert tortoises maintain body temperatures of over 100 degrees. "Ectothermic" comes from the Latin words for "outside heat," and this is a better description of how the turtle's metabolism functions. In all animals, including reptiles, biological processes are controlled by a class of chemicals known as enzymes, and these enzymes work best at rather high temperatures. In "warm-blooded" animals, such as mammals, the heat that is released during metabolism is used to warm the body and maintain the proper temperature for these enzymes, no matter what the environmental temperature might be. A human being, for instance, maintains a body temperature of close to 98.6 degrees whether the air temperature is 100 degrees or 50 degrees.

Ectotherms, however, cannot produce enough body heat metabolically to maintain their body temperatures at a specific level, and if left to their own devices would take on the same temperature as their surroundings. To prevent this and to maintain a suitable body temperature, reptiles must use external sources of heat to keep their internal temperatures high enough. That is why turtles are most often seen basking on logs or rocks in the sun; they are using the heat provided by the sun to raise their body temperatures to an acceptable level.

This variety of wild-caught turtles have made a home at Casa Tortuga, a refuge for displaced turtles.

This need to maintain and conserve body heat is one of the most important factors in any turtle's life. In hot environments, such as Latin American and African deserts, it is easy for the turtle to maintain a high body temperature; therefore, semiarid or desert areas contain a wide variety of turtles.

Because water can hold and retain heat more effectively than air, aquatic habitats in warm areas also provide the all-important external heat needed by turtles. The largest living turtles are entirely aquatic, and live either in warm, shallow rivers and lakes or in the open seas. Here the ambient temperature is so high that the turtle can afford to develop a large heavy body, something that would take an unacceptably long time to heat up if found in cooler areas.

In fact, the large sea turtles, such as Leatherbacks, have such large bodies that they can retain more body heat (which is continuously produced by the action of their swimming muscles) than they lose through their body surface. This enables them to maintain body temperatures of several degrees higher than the surrounding ocean water.

In cooler, temperate regions, such as North America or Europe, it is more difficult for turtles to stay warm. As a result, turtles from cooler areas are typically smaller and darker in color than tropical turtles (so they can absorb sunlight and heat themselves up faster). In the winter, when short days and colder temperatures make it impossible to maintain the preferred body temperature, turtles will bury themselves deep in the mud, below the frost line, and hibernate, slowing down virtually all of their body functions. These turtles emerge in the spring when the days grow longer and the temperatures get warmer.

This box turtle has developed dark markings that allow for efficient heat absorption in its cool climate.

Where Turtles Fit In

All turtles are members of the very primitive Anapsid group of reptiles, meaning that they have solid skulls with no spaces or holes between the bones. Together, the turtles make up the order of reptiles known as Chelonia, which is further divided into two groups: the Cryptodirans (characterized by the ability to pull their heads into their shells by folding their neck vertically) and the Pleurodirans (or "Side-Necked Turtles," who retract their heads under the margin of their shells by folding their necks sideways). The vast majority of living turtles belong to the Cryptodirans group.

At this point, we should clear up a matter of terminology. I have often been asked what the difference is between a "turtle," a "terrapin" and a "tortoise." The vernacular term "turtle" refers to any member of the Chelonian order—any reptile with a shell. The word "tortoise" is usually used to refer to those Chelonians that are primarily terrestrial and rarely enter water. "Terrapin" usually applies to those turtles that live along streams or ponds and are largely aquatic in their habits.

TURTLE SCIENCE

The scientific study of reptiles (and amphibians) is called *herpetology*, and reptiles and amphibians are usually referred to by experts as "herpetofauna" or "herptiles," which is usually shortened in conversation to "herps."

These names have no scientific standing, however; they are simply common names used by nonspecialists. To a biologist, there are no technical distinctions between "turtles" and "terrapins," although usually the term "tortoise" is reserved solely for the members of the Testudidine group of land turtles, and the word "terrapin" most often refers specifically to the Diamondback terrapin of the eastern United States. All of the shelled reptiles are members of the order Chelonia, and all Chelonians can correctly be referred to as "turtles."

Chelonian Anatomy

The most readily apparent characteristic of turtles is, of course, the shell, which varies from the leathery carapace of the softshell turtle, which contains hardly any bone at all, to the thick casing of the box turtle, which can make up to one-third of the total body weight. The shell is derived from bony plates in the skin that have fused to the rib cage. The internal anatomy of the turtle, particularly the breathing apparatus and the limb girdles, has been heavily modified to accommodate the shell.

THE EYES

Turtles have excellent vision and can detect motion at a considerable distance. They can also detect the outlines of potential predators, even if the intruder is not moving. Along with their keen sense of smell, turtles use their eyesight as the primary method of finding food. According to most scientists, turtles are able to see in color, and are particularly sensitive to reds and yellows (they can also sense a range of infrared wavelengths that are invisible to humans).

Turtle eyes are equipped with two large tear ducts, and in some turtles—particularly the marine turtles, which ingest large quantities of salt water with their food—these lachrymal glands are used to excrete excess salt from the body in the form of thick, gel-like "tears."

Next to their sense of smell, sight is the most important food-finding tool turtles have.

THE SKULL

As Anapsids, turtles lack the spaces between skull bones (called *fossae*) that other reptiles possess. In other animals, these *fossae* serve as conduits through which the jaw muscles are attached. Turtles, instead, have skulls that bulge out at the temporal region to provide attachment places for these muscles.

All turtles lack teeth, and instead have a sharp-edged, horny jaw sheath. Since they cannot chew, turtles must feed by tearing off bite-sized chunks of food using their front claws and their powerful jaws. Predatory turtles, such as snappers or Big Headed turtles, have sharp, hook-like projections at the tips of their jaws, shaped somewhat like an eagle's beak, to help them hold and tear at prey. Plant-eaters, on the other hand, have tooth-like, serrated jaw margins that enable them to cut and bite through tough plant stems.

THE TONGUE

Turtles, like snakes and lizards, possess a structure in the roof of their mouth known as Jacobson's organ, which is used to detect airborne chemicals. Even though they cannot extend their tongues like snakes or lizards, turtles are able to use their thick, fleshy tongues to capture scent particles in the air and transfer these to the Jacobson's organ. The Jacobson's organ is directly connected to the brain by the olfactory nerve. Turtles, thus, have a keen sense of smell, even underwater. To smell underwater, the turtle will open its mouth slightly, drawing in a small amount of water through the nostrils and passing this through the Jacobson's organ before expelling it from the mouth.

Use caution around the jaws of this common snapping turtle, especially if he is hungry!

In many turtles, the tongue is thick and immovable, and cannot be used for swallowing in the normal manner. These turtles can only swallow underwater, where they can use the rush of water to push food down their throats.

THE LUNGS

Because the shell prevents the chest from expanding, turtles must use a special set of muscles in the body to expand and contract the size of their chest cavity by moving some of the internal organs around, pumping air in and out of the lungs like a bellows. The hiss that you often hear when picking up a turtle is not intended as a threat, but is simply the sound made by air being rapidly pushed out of the lungs to make room for the head as it is pulled under the shell.

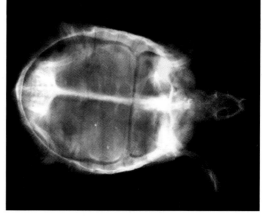

In addition, many turtles use a method of breathing called gular pumping, in which the throat is expanded to draw in air, which is then pushed down into the lungs. This throat action is made possible by the large moveable hyoid bone located in the neck. Some turtles are also capable of using the lining of the throat and *cloaca*, the cavity into which the digestive, urinary and reproductive tracts empty, to extract oxygen from either air or water. During hibernation, turtles depend completely upon gular pumping and cloacal breathing for all of their reduced oxygen needs.

This X-ray view of the Eastern box turtle shows the arrangement of the heart and lungs, as well as other internal organs.

THE HEART

Like all reptiles (with the exception of the crocodilians), turtles have a three-chambered heart consisting of two atria and a ventricle, incompletely divided by a muscular wall. The blood is pumped to the lungs by one of the two upper chambers, known as atria, and returns to the single lower ventricle. Here it mixes with the oxygen-depleted blood returning from the rest of the body. This mixture of oxygen-rich and oxygen-depleted blood is then pumped into the other atrium,

13

where it enters the aortic arches and is distributed throughout the body. This arrangement allows unoxygenated blood returning from the body to mix with the oxygenated blood returning from the lungs before it is passed on to the rest of the body.

Because of this inefficient method of distributing oxygen, turtles tire easily and cannot sustain their activity for long periods of time without frequent stops to rest.

THE SCUTES & SHELL

The turtle scutes or shell, an external bony or horny plate, is made up of the protein keratin, the same substance from which human fingernails and hair are made. Scutes are made up of living tissue and contain nerve endings (a turtle *can* feel it when something is touching its shell). The margins of the scutes do not coincide with those of the underlying bones of the carapace, and if a turtle happens to be missing a scute, the bony seams of the carapace are often made visible. Damaged scutes are vulnerable to fungal infections.

The scutes do not have a large number of pain receptors, but if they are injured or damaged, they have remarkable regenerative powers. The rings that are visible on the scutes of some turtles represent alternate periods of growth and nongrowth, and can sometimes be used to roughly estimate the age of the turtle.

The green skin color found in many aquatic turtles is actually the result of the combination of two separate pigments, yellow and blue, in the lower layers of the skin. Occasionally, turtles are born lacking the blue pigment and thus appear yellowish rather than green—these turtles are said to be "leucistic." An even rarer mutation can cause an absence of the yellow pigment, producing a bright blue turtle. Occasionally, albino turtles—those with no skin pigment—are born. The softshell turtles seem especially prone to albinism.

Commercial tortoiseshell, which was once used in large amounts for combs and other decoration, is actually the intricately patterned scutes of sea turtles, usually Green turtles or Loggerheads. The nearly insatiable demand for tortoiseshell led to widespread hunting of these turtles and their near extinction. Today, plastics made to look like tortoiseshell have replaced the real thing in most cases.

THE PLASTRON

The bottom portion of the turtle's shell, known as the plastron, is made up of four pairs of bony plates covered with keratin scutes. The plastron scutes, like those of the carapace, do not coincide with the bones of the plastron. The plastron is not dragged on the ground when the turtle is walking, but is lifted clear by the legs. The plastron scutes are constantly being replaced as they wear off. If the plastron is damaged (by being dragged over a sharp, rocky surface, for instance) the resulting wounds are easily invaded by fungus and can cause serious problems for the turtle.

In some species of turtle, such as the box turtles and the Musk turtles, the plastron is traversed by one or two flexible hinges which allow the turtle to fold its shell and enclose itself tightly within. Some turtles have gaps or openings in the bony plates of the plastron and carapace called "fontanelles" that help make the shell lighter. These are particularly large in the marine turtles, which must reduce the weight of their bodies to swim efficiently.

THE CARAPACE

The bony plates that make up the turtle's carapace develop from platelets in the skin called "ossicles" or "osteoderms," which have become fused to the rib cage and backbone. The shell is therefore permanently attached to the turtle's skeleton, and a living turtle cannot be removed from its shell. The bony plates of the carapace do not coincide with the keratin scutes that overlay them, and injured turtles that are missing scutes often show a bony seam underneath.

Because of their thickness and their vaulted construction, turtle carapaces are incredibly strong. A full-grown Galapagos tortoise can easily support the weight

15

of two or three adult humans on its shell. Despite its great strength, however, the carapace is vulnerable to sudden impacts, and can be severely cracked and damaged by a dropped object or a fall.

The Pancake tortoise of Africa is unique in having large, open spaces in its carapace. These "fontanelles" make the shell flexible, allowing the turtle to escape from predators by retreating deep into a crevice or crack and inflating its lungs to expand the shell and wedge itself tightly in a protective position.

This Radiated tortoise has a typical high, dome-shaped carapace.

The carapaces of terrestrial tortoises are high and dome-shaped. Since most terrestrial turtles are largely herbivorous, they must have large stomachs and lengthy intestines to process such low-quality food. Aquatic turtles tend to be more carnivorous, and can get by with smaller internal organs. Their shells tend to have a low, flat streamlined shape, which helps reduce drag as the turtle swims about.

The once-common practice of painting the shells of turtles can kill the scutes and infect the underlying bone, causing severe injury.

THE PELVIC GIRDLE

The reptilian pelvis is very different from that of mammals. In mammals, the legs are located underneath the body and the upper limb bones descend straight down from the shoulder and hip joints, allowing the mammal to carry its body weight efficiently atop the straightened legs. In reptiles, however, the limb girdles have joints that face outwards rather than down, forcing the upper limb bones to project out sideways instead of downwards. This means that the reptile's feet are located far out to the sides of the body rather than directly underneath as in mammals. Reptiles, thus, have a characteristic walking pose, with their legs bent out at the elbows and knees, which makes them look as if they are halfway through a pushup.

Although they have the sprawling gait typical of all reptiles, turtles have limb structures that are even more unusual among vertebrates. In most vertebrates, the shoulder and pelvic girdles are located on the outside of the rib cage. Because of the shell, turtles are unique in having their limb girdles inside their rib cage. The basic effect is a severe limitation of leg mobility (hence the proverbially slow turtle).

Despite their reputation for slowness, turtles have strong legs and some species are capable of moving quickly over land for short distances. A number of turtles, particularly those with long legs or reduced plastrons (including the Wood and Musk turtles), are excellent climbers, and can easily scale trees or even chain-link fences. Most turtles are pigeon-toed, and walk with their feet turned inward. In the aquatic turtles, the toes are webbed and the claws are long and sharp. Terrestrial tortoises have short, blunt toes and a somewhat flattened, elephant-like foot that facilitates digging and burrowing.

THE CLOACA

The cloaca is the common opening for the turtle's digestive, urinary and reproductive tracts. Aquatic turtles excrete most of their waste in the form of water-soluble urea, as do mammals. Terrestrial tortoises, which need to conserve their use of water, instead excrete their waste in the form of dry crystals of uric acid, as do snakes and lizards.

Turtles practice internal fertilization, in which the sperm is introduced directly into the female's cloaca by the male. Unlike snakes or lizards, turtles do not have hemipenes, but have a single penis, with a deep groove running down the middle through which the sperm flows. Female turtles are capable of storing live sperm for periods of up to three years, and can lay viable eggs for several years after a single mating.

Turtle egg shells are formed by a series of excretions produced by the walls of the oviduct as the developing eggs move down the reproductive tract towards the cloaca. In some turtles, the eggs are soft and leathery; in most, however, they are hard and calcareous like bird eggs. The eggs of the snapping turtle are so thick-shelled that they will often bounce if dropped. The gestation period varies according to species, but is usually between three to four months.

A hatchling takes a tentative step just moments after freeing itself from the shell.

Turtle mothers are generally good at caring for eggs. While no turtle incubates the eggs or guards the young after hatching, most turtles do take particular care in laying them in areas that are environmentally suitable and safe from predators. One exception is the Musk turtle that has a habit of dropping its eggs right in the open, which is surprising since they lay very few eggs at a time. Apparently predators don't like Musk turtle eggs very much.

Chelonian Ecology

Turtles, like all reptiles and amphibians, play a very important ecological role in a number of different ecosystems, both as predator and as prey. In some habitats, such as deserts and shallow riverbanks, turtles are the most abundant of the mid-level predators.

In most ecosystems, the largest number of living organisms are plants, which use photosynthesis to manufacture their own food from sunlight and atmospheric materials. Ecologists thus refer to plants as "producers." Because animals cannot photosynthesize or manufacture their own food, their only means to obtain food is by eating plants or other animals that have eaten plants. This sequence, in which plants make food from sunlight, herbivores then eat the plants, the herbivores are eaten by carnivores who, in turn, are preyed upon by larger carnivores, is called the "food chain."

ENDANGERED SPECIES

Unfortunately, many species of reptiles and amphibians are now becoming rare and are in danger of extinction, due largely to human activities. The Eastern box turtle, for instance, is very popular in Europe as a pet, and has been captured and exported by the thousands. Local turtle populations, with their slow aging and low rate of reproduction, cannot make up that kind of loss. The box turtles are now under the protection of federal laws and international treaties concerning threatened and endangered species.

> **DID YOU KNOW...**
>
> The box turtle can seal itself so tightly that a knife blade cannot even be inserted into the shell. These turtles are capable of staying closed up for an hour or more, without breathing, until they sense danger has passed.

Similarly, several species of African and European tortoises are similarly endangered through overcollection for the pet trade.

Turtle keepers must do all they can to protect our natural resources and our natural biodiversity. By helping to educate others about the important ecological roles played by turtles and other reptiles, and by taking steps to protect wild populations of reptiles and amphibians, we help to preserve and maintain the vast ecological web that supports all life on this planet—including ours.

Fossil
History of
Turtles

Hawksbill Turtle

Because of their thick bony shells and their compact heavy skulls, turtle remains can survive exposure to the elements much better than those of other animals, and thus become fossilized much more readily. Turtle fossils are found more often than other animals of similar size, and the evolutionary history of the modern turtle is fairly well known. The earliest turtle ancestors, however, are not often found in the fossil record, and the exact ancestry of living turtles is disputed among paleontologists.

Reptile Evolution

All reptiles are believed to have evolved from the large group of ancient amphibians known as *Labrynthodonts*. The evolutionary advance that set the reptiles apart from the amphibians was the development of the amniote egg, which could be laid on land, freeing the animal from the necessity of returning to the water for reproduction. The oldest known shelled egg was found in Texas, and dates to the lower Permian period, over 275 million years ago.

Throughout history, people have been fascinated by turtles. Here is an assortment of gem and mineral turtles collected by a proud enthusiast.

The earliest animal that can definitely be recognized as a reptile is a small creature known as *Hylonomus*, found in fossilized tree stumps in Nova Scotia dating back to the Carboniferous period. *Hylonomus* was part of the group of reptiles known as *Cotylosaurs*, or "stem reptiles," which are believed to be ancestral to all of the reptile families alive today.

Turtles' Early Ancestors

Most authorities today accept a group of Cotylosaur stem reptiles known as *Pareiasaurs* as the true ancestors of turtles. These were large, heavy-bodied reptiles that lived in the early Triassic period, just as the dinosaurs were rising to prominence. Many of the Pareiasaurs were armored by a layer of bony osteoderms embedded in the skin, somewhat like the bony platelets on an alligator's back. Over time, it is believed that these osteoderms expanded and became fused to the backbone and rib cage to form the modern turtle shell.

The earliest recognizable turtles come from later in the Triassic period, and include the extinct land turtles *Triassochelys* and *Proganochelys*. These turtles had broad, flat shells, and appeared somewhat similar to modern snapping turtles, although, unlike the snapper, the Triassic turtles were terrestrial and lived on land. Sea turtles from this period included *Plesiochelys*, which was found in Europe during the Jurassic period, and the giant sea turtle *Archelon*, which, at a length of twelve feet, is the largest turtle that ever lived.

All of these ancient turtles, however, exhibited several features unique to them that do not appear in any modern turtles. These include a series of bony projections from the cervical vertebrae in the neck (which made it impossible for these turtles to withdraw their heads into their shell) and a larger number of vertebrae than possessed by any modern turtle.

This amazing two-headed Hieroglyphic Slider is just one example of the diversity of turtle species.

The Appearance of Modern Turtles

Very early in the history of turtle evolution, the line that produced the species we know today appears to have divided into two separate groups, based on differing vertebral architecture in the neck. One group, the Cryptodirans, or "hidden-necked," developed the ability to pull their heads straight back into their shells, bending their neck into a vertical S-shaped curve. The other group, known as Pleurodirans, or "side-necked," were able to pull their long necks alongside their bodies, underneath the margin of their shells.

The vast majority of turtles living today are Cryptodirans. The Pleurodirans are a minority on most continents (they do not appear in North America at all).

Its unusually long neck has earned this turtle the name Argentine Snake Headed turtle.

The Mud and Musk families of turtles, which are closely related to the snappers and are the most primitive of the living turtles, appear to have evolved in North America shortly after the dinosaurs went extinct at the end of the Cretaceous period, some 65 million years ago. The most ancient fossils of a still-living turtle species are those of snapping turtles (*Chelydra serpentina*), which roamed over Europe, Asia and North America more than 15 million years ago.

The Testudo group of modern land tortoises first appeared in Africa, and reached its greatest diversity in the dry, arid areas of the sub-Sahara. The varied Softshell family evolved in eastern Asia but is now found throughout the world.

The most recent of the turtle groups to evolve seems to be the North American box turtles. These appear to have given up their aquatic lifestyle for a terrestrial one very recently in geological time. The Emydid family, which includes the Painted turtles, the Sliders and the River Cooters, is the largest and most diverse of the modern turtles, and seems to be just beginning its evolutionary diversification.

Living
with

part two

Turtles

chapter 3

Choosing
a Turtle

Spur Thigh Tortoise

Choosing the turtle for you depends upon several factors: personal preference as to color and size, how much space one can dedicate to keeping the turtle, what sort of climatic conditions one can provide, how often one intends to handle the turtle and whether or not one already has other turtles.

Another basic choice to be made is whether to select a terrestrial land-dwelling species (which rarely enter the water) or an amphibious aquatic species (which spend most of their time in or at the edge of the water). The procedures for caring for these two kinds of turtles are very different. In general, terrestrial turtles are easier to house and care for, but also tend to be more expensive and a bit less tolerant of changes in environmental conditions. If you intend to handle your turtles, then you can probably rule out the aquatic species—they do not tolerate handling well, and are largely for observing rather than touching. The terrestrial tortoises, on the other hand, are usually responsive to their keepers and tolerate handling much better.

Sliders are widely available and undemanding pets, and are a good choice for a first turtle.

Very often financial considerations must be kept in mind as well. While some turtles, such as Painted turtles or box turtles, are very inexpensive, others that make excellent pets, such as Matamatas or Leopard tortoises, are only rarely bred in captivity and thus are quite expensive. Since most turtles have life spans of over thirty years (and the tortoises and box turtles have been known to live for well over one hundred years), it is important to choose a turtle that you can afford to care for over a period of several decades.

In general, though, a suitable turtle for a beginning herper should (1) be docile, tame and easy to handle; (2) be of a medium size; (3) have a diet that can be easily provided; and (4) be tolerant of a wide range of environmental factors.

The Best Turtles for Beginners

Here, then, is my personal list of the best species for beginning hobbyists:

27

RED-EARED SLIDER (*TRACHEMYS ELEGANS*)

This is probably the most widely kept reptile on earth. The Red-Eared Slider is an aquatic turtle that is native to the southeastern United States. As a youngster, it is bright green with red and yellow markings. With age, the color fades to a dark olive. Adult specimens measure about nine inches long.

PAINTED TURTLE (*CHRYSEMYS PICTA*)

The Painted turtle is not as colorful as the young Red-Eared Slider, but is still attractively marked with red and yellow stripes on an olive background. There are four subspecies of the Painted turtle found throughout North America, but all have similar needs and can be cared for in the same manner. Although not quite as widely available as the Red-Eared Slider, Painted turtles are widely bred and are inexpensive.

An aquatic turtle that spends most of its time basking in the sun, the Painted turtle is a placid animal that gets along well with other species.

BOX TURTLES (*TERRAPENE CAROLINA*)

Box turtles are becoming less common in the pet trade than they were a few years ago, a result of their declining populations in the wild due to overcollection and habitat destruction. They were recently added to the Convention on the International Trade in Endangered

Species (CITES) treaty as a "threatened" species, and their export is now legally regulated. The Three-Toed subspecies, from the southeastern United States, is the one most commonly found in the pet trade, along with the closely related Ornate box turtle. Both are largely terrestrial, with the Three-Toed variety having a greater affinity for an occasional soaking. Most adults reach about six inches in shell length.

Box turtles have the longest lifespans of any animal, and commonly live over one hundred years.

LEOPARD TORTOISE
(*GEOCHELONE PARDALIS*)

The Leopard tortoise is the most widely available of the various African tortoises available in the pet trade. Other tortoises that appear on dealer lists are the Greek, the Russian and the South American Red-Footed tortoises. As adults, most tortoises reach shell lengths between one and two feet, although some species are as small as four or five inches and others reach several feet.

The Leopard tortoise is native to the dry savannahs of eastern Africa. For many years, they were exported to Europe at an alarming rate and their numbers dwindled dangerously; today, their export is regulated by international treaty, and a growing number of the specimens available in the pet trade are captive-bred.

29

Although it is a rather large turtle, reaching a shell length of eighteen inches and weights of up to fifty pounds, it is a placid and gentle creature that soon becomes a responsive and intelligent pet. They require warm and dry conditions. Captive Leopard tortoises have lived for over seventy-five years.

Like most tortoises, Leopard tortoises are almost entirely herbivorous and feed mostly on fruits and leafy vegetables.

MUSK TURTLE (*STERNOTHERUS ODORATUS*)

The little Musk turtle, at a length of four and a half inches when full-grown, barely reaches the legal limit for sale in the United States, and is in fact one of the smallest turtles in the world.

Don't let the tiny size fool you, though; the Musk turtle is a pugnacious little creature that betrays, in its appearance as well as its behavior, its close kinship with the snapping turtles. When first captured, Musk turtles will try to bite with a ferocity that belies their tiny size. They will also void the contents of their anal glands, demonstrating why they bear the nickname "Stinkpot."

Once they become adjusted to captivity, however, Musk turtles settle down into hardy and active pets. They are capable of asserting themselves even in the company of much larger turtles.

Musk turtles, are one of the few turtles that can live in a true aquarium—all water with no land area to crawl out on. They will get along quite happily in a bare tank with nothing but several inches of water and a rock cave at the bottom to sleep in.

The Mud turtle is a close relative of the Musk turtle and is sometimes found on dealers' lists. They get an inch or two larger than the Musk turtles, but can be cared for in the same manner.

There is just one drawback to this plucky little pet— Musk turtles are nocturnal, and don't emerge from their sleeping place until all the lights are out.

WOOD TURTLE (*CLEMMYS INSCULPTA*)

Without a doubt, the Wood turtle is my all-time favorite among turtle pets. This attractively colored species, about a foot long with a dark brown carapace and reddish-orange legs and neck, was once common throughout the northeastern United States, but was hunted nearly to extinction during the 1930s for use as food. Today, it is still rare and is listed in several states as threatened or endangered. It is not widely bred in captivity, is expensive and is very difficult to obtain from dealers.

This is unfortunate, for there are few pets that are as intelligent, responsive and charming as an adult Wood turtle. Their high intelligence combined with their insatiable curiosity makes them wonderfully responsive pets, who learn very quickly to recognize their keeper and can even learn to respond to their names.

Although they are usually listed as terrestrial turtles, Wood turtles spend about half of their time

31

soaking in shallow pools, and need a large water area in their cages. They are active animals, and require somewhat larger cages than most land turtles. However, they are tough and can tolerate a wide range of environmental conditions. Because they are rare and very expensive, they are not a good choice for a first turtle. But they can be viewed as the "holy grail" to which any serious turtle keeper would aspire.

Wood turtles, like these five hatchlings, are widely regarded as the most intelligent of all reptiles, and have learned to run mazes nearly as quickly as laboratory rats.

ASIAN BOX TURTLE (*CUORA AMBOINENSIS*)

These mahogany-colored turtles are imported from Southeast Asia, where they spend nearly all of their time wallowing about in rice paddies and shallow marshes. They are the most water-loving of the land turtles. Like the American box turtle, to which it is *not* very closely related, the Asian box turtle is capable of closing itself into its shell to protect itself from predators.

Although they are not often bred in captivity, Asian box turtles are imported in large numbers and are readily available in the pet trade. Nearly all of them are wild-caught and, like most wild-caught turtles, have parasites. Captive bred specimens can be rather expensive, but have better health and appearance than wild-caught imports.

The closely related Chinese box turtle is also sometimes seen on dealers' lists. It is cared for in much the same way as the Asian variety, and also makes a good addition to the turtle keeper's collection.

BELL'S HINGEBACK TORTOISE (*KINIXYS BELLIANA*)

These mid-sized tortoises are native to the arid parts of Africa and Madagascar. The Hingeback tortoise is capable of partially closing itself into its shell, but unlike the box turtle, which has its hinges across the plastron, the Hingeback's shell closes along a joint that runs across the back of the carapace. Curiously, young Hingebacks do not have a functional "hinge"—the carapace joint only becomes functional after the turtle is several years old.

The closely related Forest Hingeback is also sometimes seen on dealers' lists. It requires somewhat more humid conditions than its savannah cousin.

MATAMATA (*CHELUS FIMBRIATUS*)

The Matamata is one of the very few Pleurodiran or "side-necked" turtles found in the pet trade. In appearance, the Matamata looks convincingly like a large, moss-covered, rotted tree stump. Its triangular head sports an assortment of wavy frills and fringes, and the carapace is crisscrossed with a number of large wavy ridges. The entire turtle is nearly always covered with a thick layer of algae, which gives it a rather unkempt appearance.

Lying patiently at the bottom of a pond or on a leaf in the Amazonian rain forest, the Matamata is well camouflaged.

The algae covering functions as camouflage, for the Matamata is entirely aquatic and hunts by ambush. When an unsuspecting fish happens by, the Matamata strikes suddenly with its long snakelike neck and its impossibly large mouth.

The Matamata is a large turtle, reaching lengths of around a foot and a half, but is not very active and does not require a large tank. Because it is completely aquatic, it does not need any land area in its tank. Unfortunately, this fascinating turtle is bred very rarely, and may be difficult to find on dealers' lists (and is not cheap if you do find it). Nevertheless, the Matamata makes an interesting and unusual pet.

The Worst Turtles for Beginners
WILD-CAUGHT TURTLES

Topping the list is anything wild-caught. As the number of people enjoying the hobby of turtle-keeping has grown, so, too, have the pressures exerted upon native populations of turtles by collectors who capture wild reptiles for the pet trade. This only adds to the already crushing problems of loss of habitat and environmental pollution. As a result, the populations of many species of turtle have plummeted drastically.

It is best for all beginning turtle keepers to restrict themselves to the widely available captive-bred species until they have enough experience and know-how to properly care for the rarer wild-caughts. Even the most experienced of turtle keepers, though, should seek out and obtain captive-bred turtles whenever possible, and should make every effort to avoid collecting any specimens of any species that have been taken from the wild.

SNAPPING TURTLE
(*CHELYDRA SERPENTINA*)

This prehistoric-looking creature is common throughout most of the eastern and central United States. Although snapping turtles are very large, and can grow up to eighteen inches long and weigh over forty pounds, they are not active animals and can live comfortably in a rather small tank. They are very tough and can survive in environmental conditions that would kill most other turtles.

As the name suggests, however, adults are extremely aggressive and never become tame. Baby turtles are not usually as aggressive—but they inevitably grow into adults. Although the power of their bite has been greatly exaggerated in popular myth (no snapping turtle alive is capable of biting a broomstick in half), large adults are quite capable of removing fingers and can inflict nasty wounds.

ALLIGATOR SNAPPING TURTLE
(*MACROCLEMYS TEMMINCKI*)

These ferocious-looking turtles are the largest species found in North America and the largest freshwater turtle in the world—they can reach lengths up to three feet and weigh over 250 pounds. Although they have massively-muscled jaws and can inflict horrible bites, they are not usually aggressive. However, housing such an enormous turtle is a task that is best left to an aquarium or zoo rather than a private home.

This young lady is showing the safe way to hold a snapping turtle. As you can see, they are not a pet for beginning turtle keepers.

CHINESE BIG HEADED TURTLE
(*PLATYSTERNON MEGACEPHALUS*)

Although not all that closely related to the snapping turtle, the Chinese Big Headed turtle has the same prehistoric appearance, with a large, hooked beak and long tail. It is not as thoroughly aquatic in its habits as is the snapper.

35

Although the Big Headed turtle only reaches a size of eight inches or so, it has powerful jaw muscles and can give a nasty bite. It never really gets tame in captivity, and is a good turtle for beginners to avoid.

Softshell Turtles (*Trionyx* species)

The Softshell turtles are a widespread family that is found virtually throughout the world. They are large turtles—up to eighteen inches in carapace length—and are interesting animals with several unique adaptations. They are almost entirely aquatic, and have powerful webbed feet for swimming, but they prefer shallow water where they can rest on the bottom, occasionally extending their long necks to the surface to breathe through their elongated snorkel-like nose. As the name suggests, the carapace is leathery and lacks the bony plates found in other turtles, an adaptation that reduces drag while swimming and also flattens the shell, making it easier for the turtle to bury itself in the sandy river bottom in wait of fish and other prey.

Despite their interesting habits and unusual appearance, Softshell turtles are not suitable as pets. Although they are for the most part very shy and prefer to bury themselves placidly at the bottom of their tank, they can be aggressive if threatened and are capable of biting. With their long, snakelike necks and their quick, powerful legs, they have a much longer reach than most other turtles and must be handled carefully. They are best left to experienced turtle keepers.

Diamondback Terrapin (*Malaclemmys terrapin*)

This attractively colored turtle, with its striking black, gray and white pattern, was once widely found along the Atlantic coast in salt marshes and estuaries. Unfortunately for its well-being, the Diamondback terrapin has a delicately flavored flesh that is highly prized for turtle soups. Although some unsuccessful efforts were made to commercially farm these animals for food, they were hunted almost to extinction for the soup trade, and are now listed in several states as endangered or threatened.

In addition to its rarity, however, the very specialized habitat requirements of the Diamondback terrapin make it unsuitable for most turtle keepers. Diamondbacks are one of the few turtles that have adapted to tolerate brackish or salty water, and they do not do as well when kept in fresh water with other turtles.

GALAPAGOS TORTOISE (*CHELONOIDIS ELEPHANTOPUS*)

It may seem surprising to see these very rare and very large turtles listed as a possible pet, but they are widely captive bred for the zoo trade, and they do appear on pet dealers' lists from time to time.

This enormous Galapagos tortoise is definitely not a pet to keep in your backyard.

The Galapagos is an interesting and unusual pet, to be sure, but one that requires much more effort and room to keep than the average turtle keeper is able to give. These monsters can reach a shell length of over four feet and can weigh over five hundred pounds. Their sheer size requires that they be kept in outdoor pens year-round, and they cannot live without warm sunny conditions throughout the year. Because they are so large and heavy, and because they are avid grazers of all sorts of vegetation, they will quickly turn any outdoor pen into a moonscape, which will turn into a mud pit every time it rains.

Obtaining a Turtle

Once you've decided what kind of turtle you'd like, the next step is finding somebody who has one to sell. There are three basic sources for a pet turtle: local breeders or collectors, a mail-order breeder or wholesaler and local pet shops.

BUYING FROM A BREEDER

One of the best ways to obtain a pet turtle is through a local breeder or collector—a person who breeds a small number of turtles as a hobby. The advantages to this method are numerous: Most noncommercial, local turtle breeders are very conscientious about their animals and take extraordinary care in keeping and caring for them (if they didn't, they would have no litters of young turtles to sell). Since the breeder has a wealth of experience in keeping and raising this species, he or she will be able to answer any questions you have and pass on useful information and tips on caring for your turtle (I have met very few turtle breeders who did not relish the chance to help out a beginner). Price-wise, most noncommercial private breeders are competitive with mail-order dealers, without the shipping costs.

There are a few disadvantages as well, and they must be carefully considered. The biggest problem in dealing with a noncommercial breeder is finding one. Noncommercial turtle breeders are very rare, and are not nearly as common as hobbyists who breed snakes or lizards. Even if you live in a large city, it is unlikely many turtle breeders will live near you. And, since few local turtle breeders advertise, the only way to find them is through word of mouth. Your local herpetological society should be able to direct you to reputable breeders in your area.

Another potential problem is variety. Breeding turtles takes a lot of room and some expenditure of money. For this reason, most private breeders tend to specialize in one or, at most, a small number of species. And unless you are fortunate enough to find a person who breeds the species you are looking for, you may be out of luck.

The biggest problem, however, is that breeders prefer to sell their stock as soon as possible after it is hatched. In the United States, it is illegal to sell any turtle with a carapace less than four inches long. There is an exception made to this rule if the turtle is used for "research purposes"; regardless, a large number of breeders and dealers will sell baby turtles anyway, with the understanding that they will be used for "research or educational purposes."

Beginning turtle keepers should avoid hatchling turtles. Although they are very brightly colored and many people find them absolutely adorable, hatchling turtles are very delicate and require a lot of constant attention. They are very exacting in their environmental conditions, and demanding in their dietary requirements. Young turtles are very prone to dietary deficiencies, and can suffer from all sorts of problems if they are not fed an exacting diet. According to most estimates, over 90 percent of all baby turtles in captivity die within one year. For beginners, it is best to stick with healthy adults.

BUYING THROUGH THE MAIL

By far the most versatile way to obtain a pet turtle is through a mail-order dealer or commercial breeder. For some of the more exotic turtles, moreover, this may be the only source of that species. The addresses of several turtle dealers are listed in the Resources section at the end of this book.

The first step in obtaining a turtle through mail order is to decide what species you would like and write to the dealer for a price list to insure that he has it. Since turtles may be sold under several different names in the pet trade, most dealer lists give the Latin scientific name, and this is the name you should order by to insure that you get the exact species you want.

TURTLE BUYER'S CLUB

One option to explore if you want to reduce mailing cost is a local turtle buyer's club, in which a number of people get together and order a number of turtles that they have shipped as one order. Since the shipping charge is per box, not per turtle, this practice will lower the shipping cost per person and allow everybody to obtain the specimens they want at a lower cost than if they sent in their orders individually. Your local herpetological society can probably help you set this up.

The best way to place an order with a dealer is by telephone. The dealer will need to know what species you want and what airport you would like them shipped to (for an extra charge, you can sometimes have the package delivered right to your door from the airport).

Your turtle should arrive to you in top physical condition, just like this alert Eastern box turtle.

BUYING FROM A PET STORE

One big advantage that a local pet store has over a mail-order dealer is that you are able to closely examine the turtles before you buy them.

A good pet store should be able to point you to the local herpetological society for help and advice concerning your turtle.

If you are able to find a turtle you want in a pet store, take the opportunity to examine it carefully. Choosing a healthy turtle to begin with will save you a lot of problems, heartache and expense down the road.

Choosing a Healthy Turtle

Always handle a turtle before you buy it. (See chapter 6 for tips on how to safely handle a turtle.) This not only allows you to judge how well it tolerates handling, but it also gives you the opportunity to closely examine it for any potential health problems. The first things to look for are any sort of discharge or fluids in the eyes. If the **eyes** are not clear and bright, or if they are pasted shut, poor nutrition is the problem and you do not want that turtle.

> ## SIGNS OF A HEALTHY TURTLE
>
> clear, bright eyes
>
> nose and mouth free of fluid
>
> shell and skin free of injury
>
> firm, hard shell
>
> responsive personality
>
> regular appetite
>
> "solid" feel

The next thing to check is the **nose and mouth.** If the turtle is audibly wheezing while it breathes, or if it is breathing with its mouth open, or if you see a fluid bubbling or dripping from the nose, reject the turtle immediately. These are all signs of a respiratory infection, which is potentially life-threatening to the turtle.

Carefully examine the turtle's **shell and skin.** If there are any patches where the scales or scutes are wrinkled or missing, this indicates a burn or scar injury. Injuries to the scutes or the plastron easily become infected and can become problems later. Also, check to be sure the shell itself is firm and hard. If it feels thin, or if it gives way easily to pressure from the fingertips, that is a sign that the shell has not properly developed, probably due to a dietary deficiency.

While you are holding the turtle, look over its general **behavior and appearance.** Individual turtles do have different personalities, and one individual of a species may be shy and retiring, while another may be confident enough to walk around in your hands. Very few species of turtles will actually attempt to bite—with the exception of the snapping turtles. Most turtles will simply pull in their heads and legs when they feel threatened. If your turtle does not come out of its shell after a few minutes, it may be sick or maladjusted to captivity. It is probably best to avoid that turtle.

The **turtle's body** should also look and feel solid, and the turtle should have some weight. The skin on the legs and neck should fit snugly, without any folds or creases. If there are obvious folds or creases in the skin, it means that the turtle hasn't been eating, which may be a sign of further trouble. Since refusing to eat is a symptom of so many health problems, make sure that the turtle you want has been eating regularly and willingly. You may want to ask that the pet shop feed the turtle in front of you before you buy it.

Bringing a New Turtle Home

QUARANTINE

Because it may take several weeks for the signs of an illness to be visible, it is a good idea to quarantine any new turtle that you bring home, particularly if you already have other turtles or reptiles. Quarantining is simply isolating the new turtle for a period of time so that any potential health problems can be seen and treated. Even if this is your first turtle, you should not skip the quarantine—it is necessary to watch for signs of any impending illness.

The quarantine tank should be in a separate room from the rest of your reptile collection. Whenever you service your turtle cages for feeding, cleaning, etc., you should always do the quarantine tank last to prevent carrying pathogens or parasites from one cage to the next. It may also be helpful to keep the temperature in the quarantine tank a few degrees higher than normal.

Keep a close eye on your new turtle for a period of at least thirty days, keeping in mind all of the potential danger signals mentioned above. If you have a land turtle, be sure to examine its feces whenever they appear. If the feces are loose or watery, if they begin to develop a greenish color, or if the feces begin to take on a strong, unpleasant odor, this may indicate intestinal troubles. Also, if the feces contain a number of thin objects that look like pieces of thread, these are worms, and they will need to be treated by a veterinarian (see Chapter 7, "Keeping Your Turtle Healthy"). If your turtle is very expensive, it may be worthwhile to have a veterinarian give it a complete check-up, including a fecal exam, in addition to the normal quarantine. (New turtles, of course, should be given a routine checkup by a vet anyway.)

Most turtles that are sick will usually begin to show symptoms within thirty to forty-five days. Some turtle keepers, particularly those with large collections, like to keep their new arrivals quarantined for at least sixty days (once a disease or parasite has been introduced into a large collection, it is very difficult to contain and control).

> **YOUR QUARANTINE TANK...**
>
> This tank should be designed for Spartan functionality rather than attractiveness. For a land turtle, such as a box turtle or tortoise, a ten or twenty-gallon aquarium (depending on the size of the turtle) with a newspaper substrate, a water dish and a heating lamp and ultraviolet light will do. Aquatic turtles need a water-filled tank (containing no substrate), with a dry basking spot and full-spectrum ultraviolet lighting.

If, at the end of the quarantine period, your turtle is still healthy, active and feeding regularly, you can move it into its regular cage. After removing the turtle, the entire quarantine cage and all of its contents should be emptied and cleaned with a strong saltwater solution or a disinfectant (do not use any cleanser containing pine oil or pine tar—they are very toxic to turtles), followed by a thorough rinsing.

If Things Don't Work Out

At this point, I must introduce an unpleasant topic. It's a fact that many people buy a turtle on impulse and, after they have had it for a while, lose interest in it. Or people move and conditions at the new home do not allow them to keep their turtle. For all of these reasons it may become necessary to give up your turtle(s), and

we must examine the options you have if you must find
your animals a new home.

What *Not* to Do

One option that you can rule out right away is donat-
ing your turtle to the local zoo, unless it is a very small
zoo with a limited collection (and a limited budget).
Most of the larger zoos have strict policies against
accepting any turtles from private owners, unless the
turtle is in exceptional health and of a particularly
rare species.

Another option that should be ruled out (but, unfortunately, very many times is not) is releasing your turtle into the wild. You may believe that you are doing
your turtle a favor by releasing it to wander freely in
the great outdoors, but in reality you are probably
sentencing the animal to death, perhaps a slow, linger-
ing one. If your turtle is a tropical species and you live
in a temperate or subtropical area, the first snap of
cold weather will probably kill it. On the other hand,
if your turtle is able to tolerate the local climatic
conditions but is not a native species, it may not be able
to find a suitable food source in the wild, and may not
be able to compete for resources against the native
populations.

Conversely, and more dangerously, the turtle may
be able to compete *too* well, and may be able to establish a breeding population which will crowd out the
local species. For example, the Red-Eared Slider has
become known as the "Reptilian Norway Rat" because
of its widespread introduction to areas where it is
not native.

In addition, by releasing a captive turtle into the
wild, even if it is a native species, you may not only be
endangering the life of that particular turtle, but
possibly the lives of every other turtle in the area.
Turtles that have been kept in pet stores or in collections with other turtles have been exposed to a wide
variety of exotic diseases from all over the world.
While many turtles will be killed by these diseases,

some will not, and will carry the malignant germs inside their bodies. If these turtles are then released into the wild, they can touch off an epidemic that can decimate the local reptile populations.

For these reasons, no one should ever abandon any pet turtle into the wild. Not only is this practice thoughtless and dangerous, but in many jurisdictions, introducing non-native wildlife is illegal and will be treated as a criminal offense. (In fact, because of the danger of spreading disease and parasites, in some states it is illegal to release *any* captive animal, native or not.)

WHAT TO DO

One good option is to check with your local herpetological society. Many of the larger herp societies have "adoption" programs which can place unwanted (or confiscated) reptiles with new owners. The society may be able to find a new home for your turtle with someone who can demonstrate that they are able to give it a good home and care for it properly.

The final option, and the one most people turn to first, is to place an ad in the newspaper and sell your turtle to someone else. If you choose to do this, be selective about who you sell the turtle to, particularly if it is a rare or unusual specimen. Do not sell your turtle to anybody who is not capable of providing proper care for it.

chapter 4

Housing
Your
Turtle

Eastern Box Turtle

Housing for turtles falls into two distinct categories, depending on the species. Terrestrial turtles, such as box turtles and the various species of tortoise, require setups similar to those used for snakes or lizards. Aquatic turtles have specialized requirements of their own. We must therefore consider the housing needs of both categories of turtles.

Terrestrial Turtles

For the vast majority of terrestrial turtles, the most practical accommodation is an ordinary tropical fish aquarium. Any pet shop will have a large assortment of aquariums, and several at very inexpensive prices.

By checking the classified ads in the local newspaper, you can also usually find a number of aquariums for sale at prices far below those you would pay in a pet shop. Since you will need a rather large tank, buying it from a classified ad is probably the least expensive option. And, since you will not be filling your tank with water, it does not matter if your aquarium leaks (you might even be able to find a pet store that has a cracked or leaky tank that they will let you have at cost).

TANK SIZE

Get the largest tank you can afford. Terrestrial turtles are, on average, much larger than their aquatic cousins, and being fairly active animals, they require more room to move around than do amphibious turtles. The minimum size tank for a small box-turtle-sized terrestrial turtle is twenty gallons, and larger is definitely better. Large tortoises such as Leopards, Greeks or Red-Foots require even larger tanks.

Most aquariums come in two styles, the "high" or "show" tank, which is designed to be taller than normal, and the "low" or "breeder" tank, which has lower sides but a wider bottom area. Since turtles cannot climb the glass, high sides are not necessary, and the "breeder" style of tank provides the maximum area usable by the turtle.

Unless you will be using a lid, the tank should be a minimum of several inches taller than the turtle is long. If the sides are too low, the turtle will be able to hook its front claws on the edge and pull itself up and out. If you have more than one turtle per tank, or if you have rocks or tree branches for decoration, keep in mind that these can all serve as possible ladders for an escape attempt. For maximum security, the sides of the tank should be as high as is practical for you to still reach inside and easily clean, feed and so on. As long as your turtle cannot get up the sides of the tank, you will not need a lid to keep it in. However, if you have cats, dogs or small children, you may need a screened lid to keep them out. Several different types of screen lids are available for most aquarium sizes, and all are suitable for use in turtle tanks.

Many people seem to think that a turtle's size and growth can be limited if it is kept in a smaller tank, or that a turtle will not grow larger than its cage will allow. This is not true. Turtles, like all reptiles, grow continuously through life. Keeping your turtle in a smaller tank will not limit his growth—it will only insure that he becomes cramped and unhealthy. For this reason, it is best to provide a cage large enough for your turtle to grow into.

This Eastern box turtle is enjoying a dip in the water bowl inside its terrarium.

FREEDOM INSIDE

If there are no dangers such as stairs or heaters in the area, most terrestrial tortoises can also be given the free run of a room, as long as the air temperature is kept at a suitable level and a hot spot is provided for basking. Since tortoises cannot be housebroken and aren't usually very particular about where they relieve themselves, it will be much easier for you if there is no carpeting on the floor. Turtle droppings dry hard in an hour or so, and can then be picked up with a paper towel and flushed.

THE OUTDOOR TURTLE PEN

Another option for the serious turtle keeper is to construct an outdoor turtle pen. This project is most satisfying in areas where climate allows the turtles to be kept outside permanently; in most areas of the country winter conditions necessitate bringing the turtles inside during cold weather. If you keep turtles native to your area, however, they can hibernate naturally right inside their pen.

The pen should be large and practical, and should contain a variety of microhabitats—areas of shade as well as areas of sun. It is very important that the turtle pen have at least some areas of shade at all times during the day, as unprotected tortoises can overheat quickly in a full midday sun. At the same time, basking spots must always be available. The turtles should be able to thermoregulate by moving from sun to shade as needed.

Pictured here are components for making an outdoor habitat, including flat rocks that your turtle can sunbathe on.

Several large, flat rocks can serve as basking spots and as heat retainers. You will also need some rock caves where the turtles can retreat for shade and whenever they need to feel secure. If the bulk of the pen area is left in its natural state, with several inches of soil, some leaf litter and vegetation, the turtles will spend most of their time happily digging and foraging for invertebrates and edible plants. Make sure there are no toxic plants anywhere in the enclosure. Plants that are dangerous to turtles include such common varieties as azalea, belladonna, horse chestnut, daffodils, elderberry, larkspur, philodendron, rhododendron, yew, snapdragons, tulips and wisteria.

Since your turtles will require water, and since many terrestrial turtles do like an occasional soaking, the turtle pen should also contain a small shallow pond. Since terrestrial tortoises do not swim well and can drown quite easily, the water should be just barely deep enough to cover the turtle's legs.

The pond will lose water steadily to evaporation, and will have to be "topped up" often. It will also be soiled with dirt and leaf litter by the turtles, and will have to be emptied, cleaned and refilled occasionally—a menial but very necessary task.

The wooden planks surrounding this turtle pen protect the turtle from escape while allowing easy entry and exit for the owner.

The perimeter of the turtle pen can be made from wooden planks, bricks or stones. The wall must be at least several inches higher than the length of the longest turtle you will be keeping. If you make the wall just high enough that you can step over it, the turtles will be prevented from climbing out and you will be spared the necessity of making a door or gate for the

pen. If you are keeping Wood turtles or other good climbers, it is best to have an overhanging lip around the inside top of the wall to prevent escape.

Since tortoises are excellent diggers, you will need some provision to discourage your pets from tunneling their way to freedom. The best way to prevent escapes is to construct the entire turtle pen from wood or stone, including a full floor, and then filling in the entire pen with a foot or two of topsoil before landscaping it. Burrowers can then tunnel around to their heart's content without being able to get out.

Another method (which is less expensive and requires a lot less work) is to sink all the walls of the pen a foot or so into the ground. Although the turtles may repeatedly attempt to dig their way underneath the fence, eventually they will tire and give up. If you intend to keep the turtles in their pen year-round, there must be enough dirt and leaf litter available for the turtles to get beneath the frost line so they can hibernate in winter (more on that later in this chapter).

You can bury a shallow plastic "kiddie pool" up to its rim in a corner of the pen, and then pile some rocks or logs on one side to serve as an entrance/exit ramp.

If you live in a rural area, it is possible that your turtle pen will attract natural predators such as raccoons or foxes. If it becomes necessary to protect your turtles from these predators, you can string some wire mesh screen over the top of the entire pen, from wall to wall.

SUBSTRATE MATERIALS

There are a wide variety of materials that can be used as the substrate for an indoor turtle tank. Each has advantages and disadvantages, and each has advocates and detractors among reptile keepers.

NEWSPAPER

The most functional and economic lining is ordinary newspaper. This can be cut to size and placed in the cage, three or four layers thick, and is easily cleaned by simply removing the old layers and replacing them with fresh sheets. Because newspaper is fairly absorbent and turtle droppings do not contain much

51

moisture, it is unlikely that there will be any problem with waste soaking through to the cage floor. A newspaper substrate also makes it easy to spot parasites, as well as changes in the turtle's feces.

The disadvantage to a cage lined with newspaper is the rather "sterile" appearance of such a cage. On the other hand, newspaper substrate is plentiful, easily obtained and costs next to nothing. If, however, you would like a more natural appearance to your turtle's cage (it makes no difference whatever to the turtle), then you will need to use some other substrate.

TREE BARK

One quite usable substrate is made up of shredded tree bark or some other natural material. Among the substances offered for sale are orchid bark, aspen wood chips (not wood shavings), cocoa bean shells and ground-up corn cobs. Some keepers will use ordinary rabbit pellets as a safe substitute. These materials are relatively inexpensive, absorbent, and easy to clean—simply scoop out the feces and replace a handful of the substrate. The turtles also like them because they get to dig around in the pellets.

One disadvantage of this shredded tree bark is that if you are feeding your turtle such slimy prey as worms, the pieces of material will stick to the bark and be swallowed by the turtle. This can cause serious health problems. Another big disadvantage is that most of these materials tend to get moldy and begin to rot if they get wet from the turtle's droppings or from water splashed from the turtle's dish. These substrates must be cleaned nearly every day, and the soiled spots replaced with a bit of fresh material.

GRAVEL

Most of the prepackaged turtle kits you can find in a pet shop use ordinary aquarium gravel as a substrate. Although gravel is a workable substrate, it has fallen out of favor because of the danger that it can be swallowed by the turtle and can cause severe intestinal blockage. Gravel is not absorbent either and can be difficult to keep clean unless it is either replaced often or periodically removed, rinsed and dried.

AstroTurf

The most popular substrate is a sheet of a green grasslike plastic material known as AstroTurf. This material comes in single, presized sheets that fit inside standard aquariums, where it lies on the bottom like a carpet.

Sold in hardware, garden stores, and pet shops, AstroTurf is attractive, relatively inexpensive, and easy to use. This substrate, however, has two disadvantages. Its edges are usually rough-cut, with small plastic strings that continually unravel from the edges, and can present severe problems if accidentally swallowed by the turtle. One solution is to buy a sheet of AstroTurf that is slightly larger than the bottom of the tank, and, using a needle and fishing line, fold the edges under and sew them shut, like a hem. This prevents the strings of plastic from wearing off.

Another disadvantage to AstroTurf is that, being plastic, it is not absorbent and requires frequent cleaning. This entails dismantling all of the cage furnishings and removing the liner. Most turtle keepers who use AstroTurf will use two sheets, so they can place one sheet in the tank while the other is being cleaned.

Materials to Avoid

Substrates to definitely avoid are pine or cedar shavings, such as those used to keep mice or hamsters. The small particles of dust produced by these shavings are very irritating to a turtle's lungs and mouth, and the volatile oils that are present (particularly in cedar) can be very toxic to turtles.

"Natural" tanks, which use a layer of soil with live plants as a substrate, should also be avoided. They are difficult to clean and maintain, and turtles tend to dig into the substrate, uprooting the plants and quickly destroying the setup. Desert turtles, such as some of the tortoises, can have a substrate consisting of several inches of clean sand. The drawback of sand is that it is not very absorbent and will have to be cleaned rather often.

KEEPING YOUR TURTLE WARM

Because turtles are ectotherms and cannot produce their own body heat, they must be provided with sufficient outside heat sources to maintain their optimum body temperatures. This is the most crucial factor in successfully keeping reptiles in captivity—nearly every health problem turtles face can be directly traced to how well their thermal requirements are being met. Temperature can be thought of as "fuel"—the higher the temperature, the faster the turtle's metabolism becomes the more efficiently it can move, digest food, resist disease and perform other biological functions.

Turtles are also very susceptible to respiratory infections if they are kept in conditions that are too chilly or drafty, even for a short period of time. They must be kept warm if they are to remain healthy.

DIFFERENT TEMPERATURE REQUIREMENTS

No single temperature is best for keeping turtles. Turtles from differing ecological zones require different ranges of temperatures. Temperate turtles, such as box turtles, thrive in temperatures between 70 and 75 degrees Fahrenheit, while desert species such as tortoises need somewhat higher temperatures. As a rough average, most terrestrial turtles do well at daytime temperatures averaging in the low 80s, dropping at night to the mid 70s, with a daytime basking spot of around 90 degrees.

Specific temperature requirements for turtles will vary depending upon what biological activity the turtle intends to carry out. The turtle keeper should provide a range of different temperatures, or a "temperature gradient," allowing the turtle to select the temperature that it wants by moving from warmer to cooler areas.

The electric "hot rocks" or "sizzle stones" that are often sold in pet stores should not be used in any turtle's cage. Inability to regulate temperatures, malfunctions and risk of burns make them problematic. Hot rocks do not warm the surrounding air very much, and the only way for the turtle to obtain the heat is through physical contact with the heater. Since turtles have few nerve endings in their plastrons, it is not at all rare for them to sit unknowingly on an overheated hot rock, unaware that their skin is being severely burned. Sizzle stones are also useless in providing a workable temperature gradient and do not allow the turtle to effectively thermoregulate. Finally, hot rocks do not allow the turtles to mimic their natural behavior patterns, since the majority of turtles obtain most of their heat by basking in strong sunlight rather than by contact with a heated surface. Most turtles prefer that their heat source come from above.

It may seem to be a simple matter to place the turtle's cage near a window, where it will receive warmth from direct sunlight. However, in an enclosed aquarium, direct sunlight would quickly trap the heat and raise the temperature to lethal levels.

Basking Lamps

Use of incandescent basking lamps is one way to duplicate warming effects of the sun. (This must, however, be supplemented with full-spectrum lighting—more on this later.) The size, power and distance of the basking lamp must be determined through trial and error, and will depend upon the temperature range desired as well as the size and dimensions of the tank. For most box turtles, the temperature directly under the basking light should be in the 85- to 90-degree range, while the temperature at the far end should be around 75 degrees. Tropical turtles need basking spots of 90 to 95 degrees and cool spots in the low 80s. In most tanks, a 75-watt spotlight bulb provides adequate heat. Place the basking lamp in a spot where it cannot be reached or physically touched by the turtle, since contact can produce serious burns.

Recently, a ceramic heating element that replaces incandescent basking lights has been introduced to hobbyists. This uses a heat bulb and a socket that resembles a light bulb, but gives off only heat without light. Ceramic elements can be connected to small thermostats for precise heat control—which also makes them much more expensive than ordinary basking lights. For best results, the turtle cage should use ceramic heating elements to produce a hot spot for basking, and a full-spectrum fluorescent light to provide ultraviolet wavelengths. Both should be wired to an electrical timer, and the heater should be controlled with a thermostat. Such a setup is suitable for any terrestrial turtle.

A flat pile of rocks should be arranged directly below the basking spot, producing a localized "hot spot" for basking.

WARMING THE SUBSTRATE

Certain turtles, including desert-adapted turtles such as the Greek or Hingeback tortoise, require additional "belly heat" from an artificially warmed substrate to aid in digestion. Since electric hot rocks and heated plastic hide boxes can be dangerous, I recommend using one of two other sources.

One, the undertank heater, is constructed like a tiny heating pad or electric blanket. It is placed underneath the turtle cage, where it produces heat that diffuses through the floor of the tank and substrate. The other, heat tape, is similar, but takes the form of a long electric ribbon that fastens to the bottom of the tank. Both produce enough heat to penetrate half-inch plywood, and produce temperatures in the low 80s. Both are, however, rather expensive.

THERMOMETER

Every turtle cage should contain at least one thermometer to monitor the temperature. The stick-on thermometers used in tropical fish tanks work well and are inexpensive. Some turtle keepers like to have two thermometers, one at the warm end and one at the cool end of the tank.

LIGHT FOR TURTLES

Turtles have circadian rhythms and internal body clocks that respond to changes in daylight, and thus need a cycle of light and dark to keep all internal processes in sync. Proper lighting is also important for efficient vitamin absorption.

Turtles, like most reptiles, cannot store vitamin D3 in their bodies, and so use the ultraviolet wavelengths found in natural sunlight to manufacture this vitamin in their skin. Vitamin D3 is necessary if the reptile is to utilize the calcium content of its food to produce new bone tissue. Without a source of ultraviolet light to activate D3, turtles will suffer from nutritional deficiencies and die. They therefore need exposure to natural sunlight or to special full-spectrum lamps, that duplicate the ultraviolet wavelengths found in natural sunlight.

ULTRAVIOLET LIGHT REQUIREMENTS

Since there is no accepted standard definition of "full-spectrum" lighting, the turtle keeper must be cautious in selecting his lighting. Some companies use "full-spectrum" to refer to the presence of any ultraviolet light. The artificial sunlamps used for indoor plants fall into this category.

There are two types of ultraviolet rays: UV-A and UV-B. Plants need large amounts of UV-A, and these are the wavelengths that are found in indoor grow lights. Reptiles, need UV-B wavelengths to synthesize vitamin D3; therefore, a full-spectrum lamp specifically designed for reptiles, which emits a large amount of UV-B light, is necessary. The best advice for beginners is to stick with the full-spectrum UV-B fluorescent lamps to fulfill the reptile's needs.

The UV lamp must be as close as practical to your turtles, keeping in mind that both glass and clear plastic filter out nearly all of the ultraviolet wavelengths. Shine the UV lamp directly onto your turtles, with no intervening glass or plastic. Since UV lamps lose energy with age, they should be replaced every six months.

Sunlight

Turtles should also be exposed to as much unfiltered natural sunlight as possible. According to some estimates, a turtle gets more useful UV-B in fifteen minutes of exposure to natural sunlight than it does in several hours of exposure to artificial UV.

Lighting Hoods

Recently, special lighting hoods that contain both an incandescent heat bulb and a fluorescent full-spectrum lamp in one fixture have become commercially available. These "two-in-one" fixtures allow both basking heat and ultraviolet light to be connected to a single outlet. They are suitable for any terrestrial turtle's tank.

LIGHTING SCHEDULES

In order to duplicate the natural environment as closely as possible, turtles from equatorial or tropical areas should be provided with a twelve-hour-on, twelve-hour-off light schedule, which mimics the length of the tropical day. Temperate turtles can also tolerate a tropical light schedule; however, it is best to mimic the natural length of the day, making the photo period shorter in winter and longer in summer.

THE HIDE BOX

Turtles are well protected against predators inside their bony shells, but they prefer to have a dark retreat where they can hide and feel safe. They also need an area of shade where they can avoid overheating when necessary. For these reasons, all terrestrial turtles should be provided with a hide box.

The hide box should be snug, with enough room for the turtle to enter and turn around once he is inside (turtles cannot easily back themselves up once they encounter an obstruction). A wooden box, a little longer on each side than the length of the turtle, with one side removed for an entrance, makes a good hide box. A suitable retreat can also be pieced together using rocks and flat stones, making a shallow cave. The hide box should be placed at the end of the tank opposite the basking spot.

This Eastern box turtle is hiding comfortably in a retreat made of rocks inside the terrarium.

CAGE FURNITURE

Most turtles will do quite well in a barren tank consisting of substrate, a water dish, a hide box and a heat/light source. Such cages are rather unattractive, however, and most owners will want to include some sort of decoration or "furniture" for the turtle tank. These decorations have little use for the turtle—they are there solely for the pleasure of the turtle keeper.

ROCK PILES

Many turtle keepers like to place a small, flat pile of rocks in the cages to help retain heat from the basking light. Multicolored or unusually shaped rocks for use in fish tanks can be found in aquarium shops or your backyard. Any rocks used in a turtle cage must be smooth, as sharp, rough edges can cause injuries to the plastron and lead to bacterial or fungal infections.

Rock piles should be shallow enough so the turtle can climb on and off them easily. Most turtles can right themselves if they accidentally fall onto their backs, but some of the desert tortoises, which have high, domed shells, may not be able to. If they are trapped on their backs under a basking light, they may quickly overheat and die.

To prevent parasites, rocks and stones must be carefully cleaned and disinfected before being placed in the cage. The best way to disinfect them is to soak them overnight in a three percent solution of sodium hypochlorite (ordinary laundry bleach) or a strong salt solution. This should be enough to kill any bugs hiding within. Afterwards, thoroughly wash the rocks in a large amount of water to rinse away any trace of the disinfectant. Please note that commercial disinfectants that contain pine tar or pine oil are extremely toxic to most reptiles, and should never be used to clean a reptile's cage or anything in it.

LIVE PLANTS

Live plants are often used in the turtle cage, to give it a more natural appearance. Such plants must be chosen very carefully, since terrestrial turtles will eat a lot of plant material, some of which is extremely toxic to reptiles. Plants to avoid include coleus, crocus, impatiens, poinsettias, Spanish bayonet, trumpet vine and Virginia creeper.

Even if the plant is safe and will not harm the turtle, it is a virtual certainty that the turtle will harm the plant, either by crawling over it and crushing it or by eating all the foliage. Desert tortoises, in any case, require conditions which are too dry for most live plants, and such turtles are best kept in a bare tank with just a few rocks. If desired, some potted cactus plants can be arranged in the cage, but they will very likely be gnawed on continuously by the turtles, and will eventually be uprooted and destroyed.

For these reasons, it is best not to use any plants at all in the turtle cage. Of course, it is possible to use plastic artificial plants, which won't get eaten and can be easily rearranged after the turtle has dug them up for the thousandth time.

HIBERNATION

As we have already discussed, one of the most important factors in any turtle's life is maintaining proper body temperature. During the winter, in temperate areas, daylight hours grow so short and the temperatures drop so low that the turtle is unable to maintain its preferred body temperature, and as a result it is forced to stop feeding and retreat to an underground burrow, where its body temperature may drop to as low as 40 degrees. In other words, it hibernates (more correctly, the turtle undergoes "brumation," but "hibernation" is more common and will be used here) until warmer temperatures and longer days arrive in the spring.

Hibernation is a stressful and dangerous time for a turtle. A considerable proportion of turtles will die during their hibernation period. There are two dangers—first, the turtle must have stored enough fat over the previous autumn to carry it through the winter (since it will not eat at all until the following spring). Many turtles do not store enough fat and even though their body functions are greatly slowed during hibernation, they still don't have enough energy to make it. The other danger is that the body functions are *so low* that it is too physiologically stressful on the turtle. Many species of turtle do not require hibernation, if kept at normal temperatures throughout the winter. They will generally remain active and continue to feed (although they may eat less in the winter than they do the rest of the year).

> **HOUSING CHECKLIST**
>
> Here is what you will need to provide your turtle or tortoise with a secure home, as well as approximate prices for those items. (The prices will probably vary a bit depending on the store.) Many of these items are also available from reptile supply houses, usually at wholesale discounts.
>
> Twenty-gallon aquarium $30
>
> AstroTurf cage lining $10
>
> Ceramic heating element and thermostat $45
>
> Simulated rock water bowl, large size $10
>
> Full-spectrum lighting $15

Some turtles, however, seem to be genetically pro-
grammed to hibernate regardless of the weather, and
may become inactive even if they are kept artificially
warm. In these circumstances, it becomes very dangerous to maintain normal body temperatures, since the
turtle will refuse to eat even though its metabolic rate
remains high. This will very likely use up its fat reserves
and cause starvation before the turtle will accept food
again in the spring. If your turtle refuses to eat at all
during the winter and spends most of its time cooped
up inactively in its hide box, you will probably have to
allow it to hibernate.

*Here are some of
the items you may
consider using
when setting up
a land turtle
terrarium,
including flat
rocks, basking
lamps and a
water dish.*

PREPARING FOR HIBERNATION

To prepare the turtle for hibernation, gradually
reduce the temperature in the cage by a few degrees
per day until it is about 50 degrees. At this point, the
turtle will be torpid and unmoving. Gently place the
turtle in a box packed with slightly damp moss or towels and place it in a basement, porch or other area with
a temperature between 45 and 50 degrees (some turtle
keepers have successfully hibernated turtles by placing
them in the refrigerator). Leave the turtle there for a
period of at least ten weeks, checking in every few days.
At the end of the hibernation period, reverse this
process by raising the temperature in the tank until it
reaches normal levels. If all goes well, your turtle
should be ready to eat again within a few days of reaching optimum temperature.

If your turtles are residents of an outdoor year-round pen, they will take care of hibernating themselves, as long as they are provided with several feet of loose dirt or leaf litter to dig themselves under the frost line. During the winter, you may need to keep an eye out for skunks, dogs or other predators that may attempt to dig up the hibernating turtles.

Aquatic Turtles

Necessary equipment for housing aquatic turtles can be found at any aquarium shop as they are closely akin to the housing requirements of tropical fish.

TANK

The first requirement is a tank of suitable size. Although they will spend most of their time basking lazily, aquatic turtles are active swimmers and need lots of room. Juvenile turtles will need at least a ten-gallon tank. Adult turtles need a minimum of ten gallons per turtle. The larger the tank, the better. It is also best to use the "low" or "breeder" style of aquarium, since these maximize the surface area available.

A few turtle species can live in a true aquarium, consisting of all water without any land to crawl out on. These include snapping turtles, the Musk and Mud turtles, Softshells and the Matamata. Setting up a suitable tank for these species is simplicity itself; all you need is a tank of suitable size and, for the smaller Mud and Musk turtles, an underwater rock cave for hiding and sleeping.

In the wild, snappers, as well as Mud and Musk turtles, prefer locations with thick, muddy bottoms. In captivity, such a setup with substrate at the bottom of the tank, even gravel or stones, traps dirt and detritus and makes it more difficult to keep the tank clean. This should be avoided completely, and the tank should be maintained with a bare glass bottom.

Ironically, these aquatic species (with the exception of the Softshells) are not very good swimmers. They move around by walking along the bottom of the tank, so

63

care must be taken to maintain a proper depth of water for them. These species prefer to rest on the bottom of their tank and occasionally extend their nose to the surface (like a snorkel) to breathe. They cannot easily swim to the surface to breathe and can drown if the water is too deep for them. The water in their tank should therefore be deep enough to cover them completely, but shallow enough to insure that the turtles can reach the surface with their nose.

The other aquatic turtles are strong swimmers, and need a large deep water area where they can swim and exercise properly. The water should be at least as deep as the shell of the turtle is long, and for strong swimmers like Painted turtles and Sliders it can be much deeper, allowing plenty of room for swimming and exercise.

These are some of the components to consider when setting up an aquatic or marsh turtle terrarium, including rocks for a basking area, a heating element and thermometer, a filter and an ultraviolet light source.

BASKING AREA

Most aquatic turtles are amphibious in their habits and will need a land area in their tank where they can bask and dry off. This is important for both thermoregulation and to prevent a buildup of fungus. This basking area should be located at one end of the tank and must be big enough to allow all of the turtles to bask at the same time, but should not cover more than one-third of the tank area.

There are several ways to set up a suitable basking area. Perhaps the easiest is to pile up a number of flat rocks at one end of the tank, forming an underwater cave below and protruding above the surface to provide a dry area for basking. Line this with a moss substrate to prevent the turtles from injuring their plastrons on sharp edges as they climb on and off the basking platform.

These two young Red-Eared Pond Sliders are about to climb onto a branch in their aquarium.

A second alternative is to cut a piece of wood just big enough to fit inside the tank at water level, and use thin wedges of wood to press it tightly against the sides of the tank to hold it in place. One potential problem with this method, however, is that the wood may become waterlogged and swell up, pushing apart the sides of the tank and perhaps causing leaks.

In both of these methods, it is important that the land tilt gently into and beneath the water surface to allow the turtles to easily climb out. It is very difficult for turtles, especially young ones, to clamber onto a land surface that is above or level with the water unless there is a submerged section at the shore for them to push off from.

Some hobbyists house their turtles in an aquavivarium, in which one half of the tank is open water and the other is a landscaped dry area, using soil or some other substrate. The land and water areas can be separated by a strip of glass or clear plastic glued across the tank with silicone aquarium sealer extending about two-thirds of the way up the sides of the tank.

The larger side of the tank is then filled with water, up to the level of the dividing barrier (as in the true aquarium, no substrate should be used in the water area of the tank). The smaller portion is filled with substrate and then landscaped as a natural terrarium. Several flat rocks or pieces of wood are placed to form a ramp so the turtles can climb out of the water. These soil setups, while attractive, are not practical due to the frequent cleaning they necessitate.

HEATING

The aquatic turtle tank has two separate areas which will need to be heated—the water and the land basking area. Each must be considered separately.

The land area, where the turtles can thermoregulate and dry themselves off, can be heated using the same methods already described for the terrestrial turtle cage—an incandescent basking lamp or a ceramic heating element with a rheostat. For most aquatic turtles, the temperature under the basking spot should be around 85 to 90 degrees.

Water Heating

Undertank heaters and heating tape should be avoided in an aquatic turtle's tank, since they can present serious risk of electrocution (both to the turtles and their owner) if the tank should leak.

For some of the northern species of aquatic turtles, such as snappers, Musk turtles and Painted turtles, no heater is required for the water area of the tank. These turtles will do fine if the water is kept at ordinary room temperature.

Other species, however, including Sliders, Reeve's turtles and Matamatas, require somewhat higher temperatures, and the water portion of their aqua-terrarium will need to be heated. The best equipment for this task is the submersible type of heater commonly used in tropical fish tanks. These are glass tubes that contain an electrical heating element and a thermostat that attaches to the lip of the tank and extends into the water. The output of these heaters is usually controlled by a small knob or dial at the top. For most aquatic turtles, a water temperature of 75 to 78 degrees is suitable.

The fragility of these heaters poses a safety problem. Swimming turtles commonly knock the heater against the aquarium glass and crack it, or even attempt to climb up the heater tube and pull the whole thing into the water, presenting a serious electrocution hazard.

To prevent this, turtles must be prevented from physically touching the heating element. The best way to do this is to surround the heater with a large pile of rocks that allows water to circulate around it while at the same time screening the heater from the turtles. Another method, which can be used if the tank has a large power filter (as indeed it should), is to place the heater in the filter box instead of the main tank, allowing the heated water to flow from the filter back into the aqua-vivarium. Since most filter cases are made of plastic, though, it is important to prevent the heating element from touching the plastic and perhaps melting a hole and causing leaks.

LIGHTING THE TANK

A few species of aquatic turtles do not require any lighting in their tanks—they prefer dark or dimly lit areas. The Matamata, for instance, favors still, murky waters in shady areas, where visibility is poor and sunlight rarely penetrates. Snappers can also do without light and prefer darker conditions. These turtles get most of their calcium and vitamin D from their prey, rather than through exposure to sunlight.

Other aquatic turtles, however, require access to ultraviolet light for the proper synthesis of vitamin D3, which is necessary for intake of calcium to build shells and bones. This necessary light must be provided with the same sort of full-spectrum UV-B lamps, which were described for terrestrial tortoises. Like terrestrial tortoises, aquatic turtles also benefit greatly from small periods of exposure to unfiltered natural sunlight.

The commercial "two-in-one" hoods, which contain both a full-spectrum fluorescent lamp and an incandescent basking bulb, are useful for aquatic tanks, since they work with only one electrical cord and thus reduce the number of necessary electrical connections.

FILTERS

Maintaining cleanliness in the aquatic turtle tank is of utmost importance. Dirty tanks with polluted water not only cause a rapid growth of algae and other pests, but they are unhealthy for the turtle keeper as well as the turtles, since they provide perfect breeding grounds for the *Salmonella* organism.

Keeping a turtle tank clean is a challenge complicated by the biology of the animals. Aquatic turtles do not excrete on land, and will only void their feces into the water area of their aquarium. Most of the feces is water-soluble urea and ammonia, which cannot be scooped out as it is deposited. If soil or some other substrate is used for the land area of the tank, it will stick to the turtle's shell and feet and will be dragged into the water. Finally, if the turtles are fed in their tanks, small bits of uneaten food will remain and decay, releasing toxins and fouling the water.

For these reasons, turtle tanks must be cleaned continuously by using powerful filters to clarify and purify the water. A number of such filters are widely available in tropical fish shops, but most of these have been designed with the needs of fish keepers in mind, not turtle hobbyists. The turtle keeper must therefore be careful in choosing a filter for his tank.

The most suitable filters for a turtle tank are the power filters, which hang on the outside of the aquarium and use an electric motor to pull water into the filter through a long plastic intake tube. After passing through a layer of glass wool and activated charcoal (which cleans and purifies the water), the siphoned water is then returned to the tank through a trough or plastic outlet.

These filters are available in a variety of sizes, for differing sizes of tank. The manufacturers of these filters produce lists that tell which size filter is suitable for which size tank. The lists are calculated on the assumption that the aquarium will contain fish, however. Turtles, simply put, are much bigger and much dirtier than fish, and require substantially more filtering power. If you have one or two turtles in your tank, you should select the size filter that is recommended for a tank that is two sizes larger than yours (if you have a ten-gallon tank, use a filter that is designed for a twenty-gallon tank). If you have a larger tank with more turtles, get the largest capacity filter you can afford. If your tank is very large, more than fifty-five gallons, you may need to buy two smaller filters and run them both at the same time.

While such large filters can be rather expensive, the increased health of turtles kept in clean water, and the reduced risk of *Salmonella* for the turtle keeper, more than make up for this initial expense.

Filter Maintenance

Maintenance on these filters is a simple matter. Most use a disposable cloth pad or filter element that slips into place inside the filter box. Once this has become loaded with detritus, it is pulled out and replaced with a fresh one. Your turtle's lifestyle will necessitate rather frequent replacement of the filter elements.

Intake Tube Considerations

Power filters must process large volumes of water at a time producing a powerful flow of water into the intake tube that can be a potential danger to smaller turtles. Occasionally, a smaller turtle may venture too close to the intake and be pulled against the tube by the water pressure, where he will be pinned until he drowns. Plastic intake tubes are also vulnerable to damage by turtles that swim into them or try to climb onto them.

The intake tubes for your filter must be screened off from the turtles in a manner similar to the water heater. It is best to place the water intake tube in a corner of the tank, and then surround it with a wall of rocks to prevent the turtles from reaching it.

It is important that the intake tube of the filter reach all the way to the bottom of the tank, to siphon up all of the detritus, feces and uneaten food. Most filters come with plastic extension tubes that enable them to reach all the way to the bottom of the tank.

WATER REPLACEMENT

It is necessary to periodically remove a portion of the water in the tank and replace it with fresh water due to waste product buildup that produces ammonia toxins. For most tanks, assuming that the turtles are being fed in another container, replacing half of the water every four weeks will be sufficient. If you have a large snapper or other turtle that must be fed in its home tank, half the tank's water should be replaced every week.

The replacement water should be at roughly the same temperature as the removed portion. If it has been heavily chlorinated it should be allowed to stand in the open for 24 hours to allow any toxic compounds to dissipate.

To prevent the turtle pond from freezing completely in the wintertime, dig at least two feet deep at the shallowest end, and up to three or four feet at the deepest spot.

THE OUTDOOR TURTLE POND

Large colonies of aquatic turtles can be kept outside in an artificial pond, a strategy best suited to areas that enjoy favorable weather conditions year-round. The basic setup for the aquatic turtle pen is the same as that already described for tortoises. You will need to fence or wall in a large area with a varied microclimate, with areas of shade and sun. The walls should be as high as practical and should be sunk into the ground to discourage burrowing (aquatic turtles are not, however, as proficient diggers as their terrestrial cousins).

The water pond for a colony of aquatic turtles must, of course, be much more extensive than that used in the outdoor tortoise pen. A complete artificial pond, with the appropriate vegetation and basking spots can be installed anyplace where there is sufficient room. To produce an artificial turtle pond, an area the size and depth that you want the finished pond to be must be dug out. A good pond should be a minimum of ten feet across, with no rocks or other protruding objects left at the bottom of the hole. The center of the pond should be at least two feet deep so it won't freeze solid in the winter.

A large permanent pond can be landscaped with suitable plants and vegetation for turtles.

Once you have excavated a suitable hole, line it with a strong waterproof material, such as butyl rubber, that serves the same function as a swimming pool liner. This prevents leaks and keeps the pond water from draining away and should be as thick as practical to prevent tears. The liner should overlap the edges of the pond by about a foot with the overlapping edge covered over by several inches of rocks and soil to hold it firmly in place.

Next, fill the interior of the liner with four or five inches of clean sand, to push the liner flat against the bottom and protect it from rocks, branches, turtle claws and other potential sources of puncture. Once the liner is firmly in place, add enough water to fill the pond.

Smaller temporary ponds can be produced by simply burying a large plastic wading pool up to its rim filled with water and a pile of rocks at one side to serve as an entry/exit ramp.

The temporary "wading pool" will not be large enough to establish a natural oxygen cycle, and periodically it will become polluted with detritus, uneaten food and other wastes. The pond will have to be drained, cleaned and refilled every few months. Such a small pond will also freeze solid in the winter, and your turtles will have to be taken inside for hibernation.

This Red-Eared Slider is drying off on a rock after a swim in its man-made pond.

Shallow areas near the shore of a permanent pond can be planted with cattails, pickerel weed and other aquatic plants that provide cover for young turtles and attract insect life to the pond. The turtles can use a number of flat rocks scattered along the shore as entry and exit ramps and as basking spots. Another good idea is to place a large tree branch or trunk in the pond, so it forms a long basking platform that can be reached from either land or water. Most aquatic turtles prefer to bask on logs or branches that extend out into the water so they can dive to safety at the first hint of danger.

The area around the pond should be open and sunny for basking most of the day with plants and small bushes placed at the margins to provide some shade. Large trees should be avoided, as they shed leaves that would cause buildup.

chapter 5

Feeding
Your
Turtle

Because turtles are found in a wide variety of habitats, ranging from the open sea to arid deserts, their food preferences are wide-ranging. Some turtles are entirely carnivorous; others are largely herbivorous and thrive on plant material. In general, terrestrial tortoises tend to have different food preferences from the aquatic turtles, and in any case the process of feeding a captive land turtle is very different from that of feeding aquatic turtles. For this reason, both types of turtle must be discussed separately.

Terrestrial Turtles

Generally, terrestrial tortoises, such as Leopard or Greek tortoises, tend to be mainly herbivorous, while the box turtles and Wood turtles are omnivores and will eat both animal and plant foods.

In the wild, young tortoises are mainly herbivorous, and graze on grasses, succulents and other plants. They also will eat occasional lizards, insects and other small animals. Captive tortoises can be fed a variety of

vegetable foods, including banana, apple, melons, grapes and squash, as well as green leafy vegetables like mustard greens, escarole, kale and dandelion leaves. Lettuce of all types have virtually no food value and should be avoided.

Box and Wood turtles usually prefer more meat in their diets. In most

An insect makes a nutritious, crunchy treat for this Ornate box turtle.

species, the young turtles are carnivorous and eat a large amount of animal prey, allowing them to obtain the calcium and protein they need for proper growth and development. As the turtle ages, it begins to add more plant material to its diet, and fully mature turtles eat a mixture of both plant and animal material. In the wild, they will eat plant food such as berries, mushrooms and fruits, while a portion of their diet consists of invertebrates and small animals, including earthworms, snails, small fish and amphibians.

A good staple diet for captive terrestrial turtles is lean dog food. This should be a low-fat variety such as fish or chicken, combined with leafy greens and fruits, such as bananas, apples and melons. With some vitamin and mineral supplements, these foods provide the turtle with a complete diet.

Terrestrial turtles should also be fed as much whole live prey as possible since the viscera and stomach contents of live food provide a number of essential minerals and nutrients. Most turtles will eagerly accept fresh earthworms, either whole or chopped, and many will also take goldfish or snails. The Ornate box turtles, which are native to dry prairie conditions, consume a lot of beetles and bugs in the wild, and will often accept crickets in captivity, hunting them down one by one and eating them. Most other turtles will accept pieces of lean, raw meat, such as beef heart or liver, as an occasional treat, but whole prey is better from a nutritional point of view and should form the bulk of the diet.

This Spur Thigh tortoise is enjoying a meal of canned dog food mixed with fresh vegetables.

All turtles fed live food must be checked regularly for intestinal pests since raw meat may contain worms and other intestinal parasites. It is not unusual for turtles to become stubborn and picky about their food, accepting certain items eagerly while rejecting others. In some cases, the turtle will carefully go through his food dish, picking out all the pieces he likes and leaving the rest. To provide a varied and balanced diet important to the turtle's health, place all of the food items in a blender and chop them into a fine puree.

OBESITY

It may become necessary to strictly monitor your turtle's food intake. For most turtles, a feeding every three or four days is sufficient. Young turtles can be fed small amounts every day. Captive turtles, however, do not get the same amount of exercise that they would in the wild, and thus have a strong tendency to become overweight. Obesity can cause health problems for a turtle, and if you see that your box turtle is getting too plump, you will need to cut back on his food intake and encourage regular movement and exercise.

These three African Spurred tortoises are feasting on a commercially prepared food mix.

SUPPLEMENTS

Turtles are susceptible to vitamin and mineral deficiencies, so dietary supplements should be regularly added to the tortoise's food. A drop of cod liver oil on the tortoise's food every other meal helps add vitamins A and D, while a pinch of calcium powder adds another necessary supplement.

EATING SCHEDULES

Like all reptiles, turtles are capable of incredibly long fasts, and can go a long time between feedings. Most turtles should be fed two or three times a week. If you will be going on vacation for a couple of weeks, your turtle will be fine as long as you give him a good meal before you leave and another one when you get back.

Many turtles, even if they don't hibernate in the winter will nevertheless reduce their food intake and become inactive through the cooler months. This will do no harm as long as the turtle has been eating properly throughout the summer and fall, but you should still offer your turtle food throughout the winter.

Aquatic Turtles

Feeding aquatic turtles is a whole different ballgame from feeding terrestrial turtles and tortoises. Land turtles require nothing more than a plate of proper food from which they can graze whenever they want. Feeding aquatic turtles is not quite so simple.

In general, aquatic turtles are more carnivorous than their terrestrial cousins. The large predatory turtles, like Alligator snappers and Matamatas, are exclusively carnivorous. Both of these species have evolved specialized methods of trapping and preying on fish. The Matamata, when it senses a potential meal nearby, swells out its neck, creating a vacuum, and then opens its mouth. The resulting rush of water pulls the fish into the turtle's mouth, where it is swallowed.

This Red-Eared Pond Slider is being fed in a quarantine aquarium to avoid a messy tank.

SNAPPING TURTLES

The Alligator snapper, on the other hand, hunts by resting motionless on the bottom of a pond or river and holding its jaws open, where its camouflage shell makes it virtually invisible. Inside the mouth is a pink outgrowth of the tongue that looks remarkably like a worm, and this continually twitches and wriggles. When a curious fish approaches to investigate, the snapper's jaws close on it in an instant, pinning the prey.

The Common snapping turtle does not have a lure like the Alligator snapper, but it also depends on its natural camouflage to rest motionless in the water, snapping up any passing prey with its long, snakelike neck.

Snappers, like all other aquatic turtles, cannot use their tongue to manipulate food for swallowing, and depend on the rush of water to help push their prey down into their stomach. It is, therefore, difficult for aquatic turtles to swallow their food unless they are underwater.

The Alligator snapping turtle opens its mouth and wiggles its tongue to attract curious fish.

Eating Can Be a Messy Affair

As you can imagine, feeding is a messy affair for aquatic turtles. Since they have no teeth and cannot chew their food, turtles must tear their prey into bite-sized pieces, using their powerful jaws and strong claws. This, of course, scatters a large amount of detritus and waste particles into the tank that settle to the bottom and then decay, quickly causing intolerable odor and cleanliness problems. In a large tank with several turtles, even the most powerful of filters will not be able to keep up with the mess.

The solution to this problem is to feed the turtles in a separate container that is large enough to hold the turtle. Small aquariums make good feeding containers, but in a pinch such things as sweater boxes or large bowls can be pressed into service. The idea is to place the turtle into the feeding tank, which contains enough water for the turtle to submerge itself, and then introduce the food. The turtle is then able to rip and tear his food and make as much of a mess as he wants, dirtying up the feeding tank rather than his home tank. After the turtle is finished eating, he can be rinsed off with warm water to remove any food particles or detritus and then returned to his home tank. The feeding tank is emptied, thoroughly cleaned, and is ready for the next mealtime.

Unfortunately, the snappers and Softshells, which tend to be the messiest eaters, should not be handled for feeding. If you keep these species, you will have to use powerful filters and resign yourself to replacing the water in the tank often.

WHAT ABOUT NUTRITIONAL DEFICIENCIES?

It is necessary to supplement your turtle's diet with vitamins and minerals. Calcium, in combination with proper ultraviolet lighting, is especially important for young turtles, since it is used to produce healthy bones and shells. Whole fish, bones included, is a good source of calcium, and should form the staple diet of any aquatic turtle. Additional calcium can be provided by placing a small piece of chalk or limestone in the turtle's feeding tank, where it will dissolve and release small amounts of calcium into the water. Whenever the turtle is fed, he will swallow some of the dissolved calcium along with his food.

Preferred Foods

Probably the best food for most aquatic turtles is live goldfish and earthworms. With the viscera and bones, goldfish provide a healthy, staple diet that is usually accepted eagerly by the turtle. It is best to stun or kill the fish before feeding them to the turtles, since it may take a while for your turtle to pursue and capture its food if it is alive, and some turtles, such as Musk or Mud turtles, may not be fast enough to catch live fish. (Musk and Mud turtles feed largely on carrion in the wild.) It is best to always feed your aquatic turtles in a separate feeding tank.

Larger turtles will eat correspondingly larger fish, and for convenience sake these can be kept frozen and thawed just before feeding. It is very important that any frozen food be thoroughly thawed before feeding, as incompletely thawed food can cause severe intestinal problems.

Trout Pellets

Another good food source is commercial trout pellets, which can sometimes be found in tropical fish stores. Many reptile stores also sell commercial turtle food sticks, which are usually made from fish products. These are also nutritionally complete and do not make as much mess as whole fish. Commercial turtle foods that consist of dried "ant eggs" (actually the dried pupae) have virtually no nutritional value and should be strictly avoided, as should foods consisting of dried, vitamin-dusted flies.

Other Treats

Most aquatic turtles will also eat snails (shell and all), and these are nutritious as well as being a good source of calcium. Occasional treats consisting of raw, lean meat, such as heart or liver, can also be offered, but only rarely and never as a staple food.

Make sure your turtle doesn't have access to any toxic plants.

Adult aquatic turtles will also occasionally eat vegetable matter, and snappers are particularly disposed to eating plant food now and then. Small amounts of fresh, leafy greens such as escarole, endive, dandelion leaf or kale can be offered to any adult turtle from time to time. Like their terrestrial cousins, aquatic turtles can get by on a surprisingly low amount of food if necessary, easily going for a few weeks without being fed while their keeper is away. Although they should be fed regularly two or three times a week, they can easily tolerate skipping a few meals now and then.

Water for Your Turtle

All turtles, even terrestrial tortoises from hot, dry desert regions, should have access to clean drinking water at all times. Aquatic turtles drink regularly by swallowing a small amount of water with their food. Terrestrial turtles must have access to a water dish, particularly after they have been fed. Turtles drink by submerging their heads and using pumping motions in the throat to draw in water.

WATER BOWLS

Any bowl shallow enough for the turtle to reach into, and heavy enough not to be tipped over, is a suitable water bowl. Many terrestrial turtles also like to soak occasionally, so the water dish should be large enough for the turtle to climb inside. Since many terrestrial tortoises cannot swim at all, the water level should be just barely high enough to cover the turtle's legs.

It is important to replace the water daily. Dirty or polluted water makes a perfect breeding ground for *Salmonella* and other disease organisms.

6

Handling
Your Turtle

(Eastern Box turtle)

Since few people are afraid of turtles, it is much more likely that you will want to handle your pet turtle than you would a snake or lizard. Unfortunately, however, most turtles, particularly the aquatic species, do not take well to handling and are not very responsive to their owners. Although some aquatic turtles do become tame, and some may even learn to take food from their owner's fingers, most will make a hasty retreat to the bottom of the tank if you approach and try to pick them up.

If you are keeping a snapping turtle, you can pretty much forget ever holding your turtle (unless you want your nickname to become

82

"Three-Fingered Louie"). I have had my snapper for over four years now, and she still tries to bite me whenever I give her the opportunity. These turtles think nothing at all of biting the hand that feeds them.

The terrestrial turtles, on the other hand, seem to be much more intelligent than their aquatic counterparts, and often become very responsive toward their keepers. My Wood turtle follows me around like a puppy dog, often clawing at my shoes to get me to rub his head or scratch his shell (or, more often, to give him a tidbit of whatever I am eating).

Even though turtles are well protected in their shells, they are susceptible to injury if not properly handled. Some turtles are capable of causing injury to their keeper if they are handled incorrectly.

Holding Your Turtle

The best way to hold most turtles is to grasp the shell gently but firmly at the sides with your fingers, at the same time allowing the turtle's feet to rest in the open palm of your other hand. If the turtle gets excited, he will make kicking or swimming motions with his feet and legs, but he will not escape as long as you are gripping his shell. With larger turtles, you will need to use both hands, one on each side of the shell, extending your fingers underneath the plastron to support the turtle's weight. This will leave the feet dangling, however, which the turtle may not particularly like. When holding any turtle, watch out for the feet—turtles have sharp claws and may scratch you if they begin flailing their limbs in an effort to get down.

> **CHARACTERISTICS OF YOUR TURTLE/TORTOISE:**
>
> Long-living
>
> Independent
>
> Inquisitive
>
> Adaptable
>
> Hearty Appetite

For the most part turtles should be carried around as little as possible. Aquatic turtles do not like being held or handled, and tend not to be very playful or sociable pets. Tortoises and terrestrial turtles sometimes enjoy having their head or neck rubbed or their shell patted, but they also prefer to keep all four legs firmly on the ground.

Transporting a Turtle

Sometimes, of course, it becomes necessary to transport a turtle, either for a visit to the vet or for use in a talk or educational show.

Give your turtle a feeling of security by supporting its weight, even if it only takes a couple of fingers (as is the case with this young Pond Slider).

SNAKE BAG

Very small turtles can be transported using a snake bag. This is simply a large cloth bag, about 18 inches long and a foot or so wide (a pillowcase makes a good improvised snake bag). The little turtle is placed into the bag along with a handful of damp paper towels. The top portion of the bag is then twisted tightly and tied in a loose overhand knot to then conveniently carry around. Since the weave of most cloth bags is not airtight, the turtle will be able to breathe right through the bag. Be careful that nobody steps or sits on the bag.

Larger turtles usually can't be bagged since their sharp claws can make quick work of the cloth and they will easily shred their way to freedom. They can be safely transported in a box that has been securely taped closed and has had a number of air holes punched in the sides. The box should also contain wads of newspaper or rags to prevent the turtle from being bounced around too much during the trip. Make sure that the air temperature in the car is warm enough for the turtle. If you are transporting a large snapper or Softshell, it is best to use a wooden box rather than cardboard.

Don't underestimate the stimulation your turtle may need. Some turtles prefer a lot of independence, while others don't mind supervised social time with other family pets.

Are Turtles Intelligent?

The structure of a turtle's brain is somewhat similar to that of a bird, but the turtle, like all reptiles, lacks the greatly enlarged cerebral hemispheres found in birds and mammals. Since these are the areas of the brain that control learning and reasoning, most turtles don't share the intelligence of warm-blooded creatures.

Some turtles are no intellectual slouches, though, at least not compared to other animals. In some species, the brain reaches a size relative to the body weight that is comparable to birds, and these turtles, while unable to approach the brainier mammals, nevertheless seem to have mental faculties that function on the level of birds.

The Brainiest Turtle The most intelligent turtle is reputed to be the Wood turtle, which has been the subject of laboratory tests and experiments. In controlled experiments

THE GREAT TURTLE ESCAPE

Once I captured a rather large snapping turtle crossing a local road and, having nothing else handy, put her in a large snake bag before tossing her in the back of my station wagon. About a mile down the road, I saw a large dinosaurian head peering at me over the back seat, where the thoroughly annoyed turtle was standing on the now-shredded bag. I broke a few speed limits driving home, with one eye on the road and one anxious eye on the floor underneath me.

using food rewards, Wood turtles can learn to run a maze almost as quickly as laboratory rats. They can also retain this learning for a period of several weeks, and can successfully recall mazes they had not been exposed to for some time.

SPATIAL SENSE

One series of experiments has centered around the spatial sense of various turtles. In these experiments, a deep hole in the floor was covered over with a clear sheet of glass, and various types of animals were released at the edge of the "cliff." Less intelligent animals, such as certain lizards, did not hesitate when they reached the cliff edges, and ran right across the glass—presumably, had it been a real cliff they would have unthinkingly plunged to their doom. Visually oriented mammals, such as rats, approached the edge of the simulated cliff with caution, and refused to step beyond it onto the glass.

Interestingly, aquatic turtles such as Painted turtles took no notice of the cliff, and scrambled at top speed right across the glass. Terrestrial turtles, however, such as box turtles, did not venture beyond the edge.

Beware of your turtle plotting a clever escape . . . this box turtle has figured out how to get out of an outdoor habitat.

The explanation for this behavior seems to be that aquatic turtles are accustomed to basking over water, where they can safely dive from a height to escape predators. Thus they have no need for highly refined spatial abilities.

I believe the reason for differences in spatial abilities may lie in the feeding habits of these turtles. The box turtle does most of its feeding on land, eating vegetation and small invertebrates that cannot run away and hide. The Wood turtle, on the other hand, finds a large portion of its food in the water, particularly small frogs and fish that can swim away and attempt to hide behind rocks or branches. It would therefore be advantageous for the Wood turtle to be able to mentally "track" fleeing prey, remembering where it disappeared and then following it back to its hiding place to flush it out. This behavior might be expected to produce a more highly developed spatial ability in the Wood turtle.

Terrestrial box turtles have a developed sense of spatiality in order to avoid cliffs and other dangerous falls.

LEARNING ABILITY

In captivity, many turtles display the ability to learn. Aquatic turtles that are fed at the same time every day soon learn when it is feeding time, and will be ready and waiting when their keeper approaches. Tame turtles will also be able to distinguish their keeper from others, and will often swim to them to be fed. The terrestrial tortoises learn even more quickly who their keeper is, and often display an inclination to follow him around.

From the size of this Eastern box turtle's yawn, you can see that even turtles have the ability to be bored!

The more intelligent turtles can learn to respond to their names, making them a sort of reptilian prodigy. Thus, while your turtle will never learn to do tricks or to fetch the newspaper, he may be able to at least recognize who you are and respond to you.

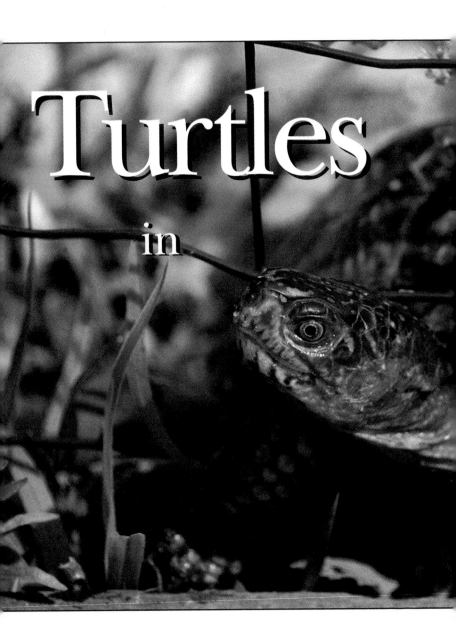

Turtles

in

part three

Our
World

chapter 7

Keeping Your Turtle
Healthy

Box Turtle

In general, turtles are quite hardy animals and, provided they are being kept in proper conditions, are unlikely ever to present you with urgent medical problems. However, captive turtles are subject to a number of ailments, several of which can be life-threatening if not promptly identified and treated.

Finding a Veterinarian

Finding a good veterinarian for your turtle may be one of your most difficult tasks. While most vets are well trained in small animal care, only a few have had any training in the unique medical requirements of reptiles and amphibians. As a result, most veterinarians will flatly refuse to examine your turtle. Some who decide to try may have no practical experience whatsoever with reptiles, and very little training beyond a single course or two in herp anatomy and physiology. Keep in mind, that unless you live in or near a large urban area, you are unlikely to find a vet who has had any realistic training in reptile care.

How to Find a Suitable Veterinarian

The first choice is to approach your local herpetological society for help. Not only does your local herp society deal with qualified veterinarians all the time, in matters such as adoptions and rescues, but most of the competent reptile vets are likely to be members of the herp society, as well. Another choice, if you have a local wildlife rehabilitation center or zoo nearby, is to ask for their help—they might be able to point you to a good herp vet. The final option is to call any veterinarian in the phone book and ask for a recommendation of a good reptile veterinarian.

Give yourself time to do extensive research to find a veterinarian qualified to care for your turtle.

The Checkup

Once you have found a suitable vet, it is a good idea to make an appointment for a checkup. This allows you to get to know the vet, and your vet to get to know your turtle. The vet will examine your turtle for external parasites and the most common diseases. He will also probably weigh your turtle and measure it.

91

If your turtle is maintained under proper conditions, it is unlikely that he will ever need more than an annual checkup from the vet. However, problems can arise, and you should be able to recognize the onset of a condition, deal with a minor problem and determine if your turtle needs to get to the vet.

Salmonella

The health concern that comes up most often when discussing turtles, ironically, does not usually affect the turtle at all—instead it attacks the turtle's owner. The incidence of *Salmonella* disease from pet turtles is often overblown and exaggerated (many more people get the disease from handling raw chicken than from handling pet turtles). Nevertheless, it is a fact that the *Salmonella* organism, which can produce severe gastrointestinal disease, can be found living naturally on the shells and skin of turtles, particularly aquatic turtles. Under natural conditions, *Salmonella* never builds

Save your turtle's most recent fecal dropping, place it in a sealing bag, and bring it along on your turtle's checkup. The vet will examine it for worms and other parasites.

up to a level where it can produce infections. In captivity, however, particularly where the tank is not being kept properly cleaned, the *Salmonella* population can explode and congregate in the water. From there it is transferred to the turtle's shell and skin, and then transferred to the owner's hands.

It is illegal to sell any turtle in the United States that has not been certified as being free of *Salmonella*. To eliminate the bacteria, most turtle breeders treat their tanks with the antibiotic gentamicin. Unfortunately, however, this has now produced a drug-resistant strain of *Salmonella*—a serious matter, since gentamicin is also the drug used to treat human victims of *Salmonella* poisoning. Since it is impossible to kill all of the bacteria, it is a safe assumption that any turtle you see will have at least some *Salmonella* organisms living on its shell.

In an aquatic turtle tank, an efficient filtration system using activated charcoal is absolutely vital to remove waste products, uneaten food and other pollutants that can encourage the growth of the bacteria—but it does not eliminate the necessity of periodically replacing a portion of the water. (If you feed your turtles in a separate container, controlling bacteria in the main tank becomes much easier.) Incidentally, raw chicken is an excellent source of *Salmonella* bacteria, and should be strictly avoided as a food for any captive turtle.

Fortunately, a few simple precautions can virtually eliminate the danger of contracting a *Salmonella* infection from a captive turtle. First, always wash your hands after handling any reptile or anything from a reptile's cage. Although washing with plain water is ineffective, washing with soap will kill the *Salmonella* organism. Second, be sure that your turtle's cage is kept clean, that feces are removed promptly, and that the water is changed often. Third, never allow a reptile to come in contact with any surface that is used for human food preparation, such as kitchen counters, sinks or food dishes, and make sure you wash your own hands before touching any such surfaces yourself. Fourth, always supervise small children when they are near the turtles. Do not let them put their fingers in their mouths while handling the turtle, and make sure they wash their hands promptly afterwards. If these simple rules are followed, it is unlikely that you will ever have any *Salmonella* problems with your reptiles.

> ### SALMONELLA STOPPERS
>
> Always *wash your hands* after handling any turtle.
>
> *Use soap*, it kills the *Salmonella* organism.
>
> Be sure that your turtle's water (aquatic or terrestrial) is always clean and changed often, to prevent the bacteria from building up.
>
> *Supervise small children when they are near a turtle*. Do not let them put the turtle in their mouths, or put their fingers in their mouths after handling the turtle.
>
> If these simple rules are followed, it is unlikely you will ever have any *Salmonella* problems with your turtles.

Wounds

Minor wounds and scrapes can be treated by dabbing some antibiotic cream such as Neosporin, which can be found in any drugstore, onto the injury. Turtles, like most reptiles, have very good internal healing mechanisms, and most minor injuries will heal themselves in a few weeks.

If the turtle is improperly housed, it can receive minor burns from a heat lamp or a sizzle stone. These can also be treated with antibiotic cream.

Although turtles are not usually aggressive animals, larger turtles will sometimes attempt to intimidate smaller ones by biting.

Creams such as Neosporin, however, are not of much use with aquatic turtles, since they are quickly washed off. Aquatic turtles that have suffered a minor wound should be soaked in a separate tank containing a liquid solution of antibiotic such as Betadine, which can usually be found at the drugstore. A ten-minute soaking twice a day is sufficient for most minor injuries. The turtle should be rinsed off before being returned to its normal tank.

Respiratory Infections

Signs of a respiratory infection are runny eyes, discharge from the nose, gasping or wheezing breaths, and breathing with the mouth open. This problem is nearly always the result of environmental conditions that are too cool or drafty. Turtles from desert or tropical regions can develop colds if they are chilled for even a very short period of time. Untreated, the infection can spread to the lungs and cause a fatal case of pneumonia.

If the infection is not severe, it can usually be cleared up by raising the temperature in the turtle's tank by five or ten degrees for a few days. If the symptoms persist, or if the turtle begins having noticeable difficulty breathing, then it's time for a trip to the vet. Most respiratory infections are treated with antibiotic injections. Your vet will give you a supply of needles and show you how to administer the shots. The treatment usually lasts about three weeks.

Intestinal Infections

There is no mistaking the symptoms of an intestinal infection. The turtle will void smelly, slimy feces, which are watery and loose. Aquatic turtles will quickly turn their tanks into a cesspool, while terrestrial turtles will have you working overtime cleaning their substrate.

There are two possible culprits, and it usually takes a veterinarian to determine the actual cause of infection. One possibility is that protozoans have infected the intestinal lining. Another is that *Salmonella* bacteria may have built up in the water to such high levels that they have infected the turtle. (This is a certain indication that the tank has not been kept sanitary.) The latter is more complicated to treat due to drug-resistant strains of *Salmonella*.

> **TIPS FOR CHOOSING A VETERINARIAN**
>
> Select a vet before bringing your turtle home
>
> Ask friends for recommendations
>
> Check with a local herp society
>
> Ask if the vet is a member of the Association of Reptile and Amphibian Veterinarians
>
> Feel free to ask questions and seek second opinions

Whatever the cause, intestinal troubles can kill a turtle quickly. If you ever see your turtle having intestinal problems, get him to a vet immediately for a culture and proper treatment.

Internal and External Parasites

Parasites are not usually found in captive-bred turtles, but are fairly common in wild-caught individuals (particularly imports). Because turtles live in water, and most of their food consists of aquatic prey such as fish, worms and snails, they are more susceptible to parasites.

LEECHES

The most common external parasites are leeches, resembling small dark worms that attach to skin at the turtle's neck or legs. They live by sucking blood from their host, and although they are hardly ever found on terrestrial turtles, they are common on wild-caught aquatics. The best treatment is to carefully remove the leech with a pair of tweezers and then wipe the area with a disinfectant or antibiotic cream.

LIVER FLUKES

A number of internal parasites can infest turtles. The most common are liver flukes, which are found in snails and are passed on to the turtle with its food. Nearly any wild-caught turtle you receive will be infested with flukes. Usually, they do no great harm, but very heavy infestations can destroy the internal organs and kill your turtle. The symptoms are loss of appetite and rapid weight loss. Severe infestations must be treated by a vet.

INTESTINAL WORMS

If your turtle seems to be eating a lot but not gaining weight, it may have intestinal worms such as nematodes. Nearly all wild-caught turtles are regularly exposed to these parasites, and all wild-caught specimens will probably be infected. Most internal parasites that attack turtles have complex life cycles, parts of which are spent inside snails, fish or worms. Usually, the eggs are passed in turtle feces and ingested by snails, where they hatch. The young nematodes are then swallowed by the turtle when it feeds on the snail, entering the digestive tract to begin the process again. Even if your turtle is captive-born and unexposed to the wild, he may contract parasites through eating contaminated food.

For this reason, both wild-caught and captive-bred turtles must be examined regularly for the presence of worms or parasites. You may see worms in the turtle's feces—they look like tiny bits of thread. The worms can weaken the turtle by robbing him of nutrients. Heavy infestations can damage the intestines or other internal organs.

If you suspect that your turtle has worms, you must take a recent fecal sample to your vet and have it examined. Intestinal worms can be treated with a dewormer, which is usually slipped to the reptile in its food or given as oral drops.

Cloacal Prolapse

Prolapses occur when the lining of the cloaca protrudes from the anal opening and is exposed outside the body. In some cases, part of the small intestine may also be exposed, and in female turtles the ovaries may also be extended. Although prolapses are horrifying to look at, they are not usually life-threatening

If your turtle has a prolapsed rectum that doesn't correct itself in a few days, see the veterinarian.

or painful to the turtle. The cause of cloacal prolapse is not known—it may be a combination of several factors, including stress or the presence of intestinal worms.

If your turtle suffers a prolapse, it is very important to keep the protruding organs moist. With an aquatic turtle, of course, this presents no problem; terrestrial turtles, however, should be placed in a bowl of shallow water to keep the organs damp. If the prolapsed tissues dry out, they will die, and it will become necessary for a veterinarian to remove the dead tissues surgically.

Usually, if the turtle is enticed to move around a bit, the prolapse will work itself back in. If necessary, you can gently massage the areas surrounding the protrusion, but you should never attempt to push or force the organs back in. Most often, the prolapse will correct itself after a few days. If it doesn't, it's time to see the vet.

It is also important to watch that the turtle does not interfere with the prolapse by clawing at it. The turtle is unable to recognize that the prolapse is a part of his own organs, and may make an effort to detach the "foreign object" from his tail. In addition, other turtles in the tank may attack the prolapse. If a turtle is able to reach the tissue, he can turn it into a bloody mess in a short time. If that happens, surgery will probably be necessary.

Although cloacal prolapses are not all that common, some individual turtles seem to be prone to them, and may experience prolapses several times within a short period. In this case your vet may stitch the cloacal opening to make it tighter and prevent further recurrence.

Visceral Gout

This is a dietary disease that is usually produced by high-fat. Like most reptiles, turtles cannot digest animal fat very efficiently, and a steady diet of fatty food can cause uric acid crystals to build up in the kidneys and other internal organs. This causes these organs to literally become rock hard and to stop functioning, which can cause very sudden death.

The disease can be prevented by feeding a proper diet and by limiting the intake of red meat, which is often too high in fat. If you are feeding your turtles canned dog or cat food, make sure that these are made largely with lean meats, such as fish or chicken.

Skin and Shell Problems

ALGAE

After a time, your aquatic turtle may begin to sport a rather unattractive coating of green slimy substance, which may also begin to cover the inside of the tank and other exposed surfaces. Occasionally, it may become so thick that the water itself will turn bright green, making it impossible to see anything inside the tank. This is algae, and it is completely harmless to the turtle (although it will probably drive the turtle keeper nuts). In the slower-moving aquatic turtles, like snappers and Matamatas, a thick heavy coat of algae serves as camouflage for their ambush style of hunting.

A buildup of algae in the tank should *not* be treated with chemical algicides, as most of these contain hydrochloric acid, which can be harmful to the turtles. Lessening the period of time during which the light is on helps reduce algae growth. Some hobbyists keep a number of large snails or algae-eating fish in the turtle tank for the express purpose of grazing all the algae, but the presence of these animals will complicate the task of keeping the tank clean, since they contribute additional waste products. The best way to prevent a buildup is to periodically change a portion of the tank water, which should be done as a matter of routine.

The green splotches on this Western Painted turtle's shell indicate algae buildup.

Fungus

If instead of slimy green splotches you begin to see cottony white tufts on the turtle's shell or skin, then it is time to worry. This is fungus, and it usually attacks the turtle at a site where the skin or scutes have been injured. Since most turtles prefer warm, damp conditions that favor fungal growth, fungal spores are always present and waiting for an opportunity to invade. If the fungus gets underneath the scutes, it can penetrate the carapace or plastron and produce large gaping holes, a condition known as ulcerative shell disease.

Eventually, the fungus will enter the body cavity, which will be fatal to the turtle.

Fortunately, fungal infections are easily treated. The best remedy is to place the infected turtle in a weak solution of iodine for a ten-minute soak, twice a day. Between treatments, keep the turtle dry and maintain a slightly higher temperature in its environment. To help prevent fungal infection, insure that the turtle has a dry and warm area in the tank for basking, where it can dry off completely. Even in aquatic tanks, the land area must be bone dry. Damp conditions can lead to fungal infections.

Beginners will probably want to have a veterinarian trim their turtle's beak and claws.

Beaks and Claws

Unlike snakes and lizards, which shed their skin in large flakes or all in one piece, turtles replace their skin gradually by continuously flaking off tiny pieces. Thus, turtles are not prone to the shedding problems that can affect other reptiles. However, captive tortoises are prone to one problem that lizards or snakes never face. The turtle's horny jaw sheaths grow continuously throughout life, as do its claws—much like human fingernails.

Captive turtles are not always able to wear down their beaks and claws quickly enough. In order for the turtle to walk and chew properly, it may sometimes be necessary to have a veterinarian trim its beak and claws.

Nutritional Problems

The most common ailment is characterized by refusal to eat and swollen eyelids, which can lead to permanent eye damage and blindness. This is caused by a deficiency of vitamin A in the diet, which is not a serious disorder if treated promptly. Your vet will give the turtle an injection of a vitamin A supplement, and may also apply some medicated eye drops to clear up the problem. This condition is best prevented by feeding a proper diet, one including a number of leafy green vegetables high in vitamin A. Carnivorous turtles can be dosed with vitamins by occasionally placing a few drops of cod liver oil in their food.

This box turtle is eating a healthy variety of vegetables, which is important since captive turtles are very susceptible to dietary deficiencies, and nutritional problems are probably the leading cause of death.

Young turtles are particularly susceptible to calcium deficiencies, manifested by soft, rubbery shells and malformed limbs. This is nearly always the result of an improper diet, but can also be produced by insufficient vitamin D3 due to a lack of exposure to ultraviolet B wavelengths.

Treatment consists of calcium supplements and increased ultraviolet light, but if the condition persists, it can lead to permanent deformities or even death. The best prevention is a proper diet, with calcium supplements and calcium-rich foods, such as whole fish.

The disease can also be avoided by providing adequate access to unfiltered natural sunlight or, failing that, to an artificial UV-B lamp.

8

Turtles
and the Law

Until about thirty years ago, there were virtually no laws regulating the capture or sale of wild animals. Individuals or businesses were free, within the limits of "animal cruelty" laws, to capture, export or import and sell any species desired. The unfortunate result was the decimation of many species of wildlife, including reptiles, and the hunting of other species to near extinction.

In the 1960s and early 1970s, the growing environmental movement made most people aware of the tremendous damage that humans were doing to our world ecosystems. In this period, a number of laws were passed to protect threatened or endangered species and to regulate the sale and possession of many types of native wildlife.

Most of these laws are still in effect, and may have an impact on the amateur turtle keeper or hobbyist. Because there are so many differing state and local laws, this book cannot serve as a guide to the legalities of turtle-keeping. The best it can do is provide a broad overview—it is the responsibility of the individual turtle keeper to know and obey all applicable legal restrictions.

A variety of protected turtles enjoying a pond at a Georgia turtle farm.

International Laws

Without question, the single most important international agreement affecting reptile keepers and hobbyists is the Convention on the International Trade in Endangered Species (CITES), also known as the Washington Treaty, signed in 1973 and ratified by the United States in 1975. Over 120 nations have joined in signing.

Under CITES, protected animals are divided into two groups. Animals listed under CITES Appendix I are those in immediate danger of extinction. It is illegal to import or export any of these animals, except for zoos under special permit.

CAPTURING TURTLES

It is easy to forget that wild animals, after being free in their natural habitat, do not appreciate captivity. Remember that it is illegal and prosecutable under state and federal laws to remove such animals. Think about the kind of unhappy pet this type of turtle would make and the risk you are taking if you capture one. Is it worth it?

Animals listed under CITES Appendix II are not yet in imminent danger of extinction, but are declining rapidly and must be given protection. It is illegal to import or export any of these species unless they were captured under a special permit or unless they were captive-bred.

The primary purpose of CITES is to prevent international smuggling of endangered or threatened animals taken from the wild. Wildlife smuggling is a serious problem; according to some Interpol estimates, illegal wildlife trade is a $6 billion a year business, placing it just behind illegal drug trafficking and just ahead of illegal arms smuggling.

Federal Laws

The most important of the federal laws pertaining to the collection and raising of turtles and other reptiles is the Endangered Species Act, passed in 1973, shortly after CITES was signed.

The photo of this Plowshare or Angonoka tortoise was taken in Madagascar. This is one of the world's rarest tortoises, and is legally protected from exportation.

ENDANGERED SPECIES ACT

The stated purpose of the **Endangered Species Act** is "(1) to provide a means whereby the ecosystems upon which endangered species depend may be conserved, (2) to provide a program for the conservation of such endangered and threatened species."

Under the ESA, animals (and plants) that are vulnerable to extinction are listed in two categories. The most seriously vulnerable are listed as "endangered species," defined as "any species which is in danger of extinction throughout all or a significant portion of its range." It is illegal to disturb, collect, possess or sell any of these species.

Organisms not yet endangered but in jeopardy of becoming so in the near future are classified as "threatened," which is defined as "any species which is likely to become an endangered species within the foreseeable future throughout all of a significant portion of its range." Threatened species may be collected, captive bred and sold, but only under stringent permits that specify legal limits on such collection. Anyone in possession of a threatened species should be able to show that the animal was obtained legally.

Circumstances under which the Endangered Species Act are likely to apply to most turtle collectors would be if they capture their own turtles in the wild or purchase a turtle that is listed as "threatened" or "endangered" from a breeder. Most responsible turtle keepers refrain from collecting wild turtles at all, preferring to keep them in the wild where they belong, instead buying captive-bred turtles. However, if you do choose to capture a turtle from the wild, be absolutely positive that it is not a species that is protected under the Endangered Species Act. If you purchase a species that is listed under the ESA, ask for the appropriate documentation to show that your turtle was obtained legally. Any legitimate breeder of endangered or threatened species will do this routinely.

> **HELP PROTECT TURTLES**
>
> Start with abiding by conservation legislation—hobbyists and collectors should absolutely refuse to buy any imported wild-caught reptiles, and should not purchase any turtle which was not captive-bred in the United States. You can also check out herp groups in your community and get involved in local efforts; small actions can produce great results!

LACEY ACT

Another federal law that may apply to turtle keepers is the Lacey Act, which makes it a misdemeanor to transport any animal obtained illegally across state lines. If you illegally capture a turtle in New Jersey, for instance, where permits are required to take most turtles from the wild, and transport it to Pennsylvania and sell it, you are in violation of federal law.

Again, the only way this law applies to you is if you have captured a turtle in the wild and are attempting to sell or give it to someone in another state. If you are going to capture turtles from the wild, you must make yourself familiar with all of the applicable laws and regulations in your state.

A striking example of a Three-Toed box turtle, considered to be endangered in certain states.

It is also illegal to collect or remove any animal or plant, regardless of its standing under the ESA, from within a national park, national wildlife refuge or other federal territory.

SALES AND POSSESSION RESTRICTIONS

Finally, there are federal laws that apply specifically to the sale and possession of turtles. During the 1960s, when baby Red-Eared Sliders were being sold by the hundreds of thousands (and kept in what, for the most part, were appalling and quickly lethal conditions), several states raised concerns about the transfer of *Salmonella* from turtles to children. A few states passed laws making it illegal to sell any turtle at all; several others passed restrictions on the size of turtle that could be sold.

In 1975, the federal government, after concluding that almost a quarter million cases of *salmonellosis* a year were caused by improperly kept turtles, stepped in and banned the sale of any turtle with a carapace under four inches in length (an exception was made for baby turtles to be used for "research and education purposes"). Turtles over four inches long, it was assumed, would cost more to buy and thus create a greater incentive for owners to keep and maintain in sanitary conditions, thereby helping to control the *Salmonella* problem.

Here are two immature Florida snapping turtles, one is albino. The sale of reptiles in Florida, including these, is largely unregulated.

Today, the information on how to avoid the unsanitary conditions that lead to *salmonellosis* outbreak is widely available, and the number of disease cases which can be traced to captive reptiles is extremely low. Nevertheless, the federal restrictions still apply.

In Connecticut, where the Bog turtle is listed as an endangered species, owners of legally obtained Bog turtles must register them with the state

State Laws

State laws affecting reptile keepers fall into two distinct categories—laws that regulate and control the capture and sale of native species, and laws that regulate or limit the types and number of turtles kept within the borders of that state.

107

For the most part, laws pertaining to the collection of native turtles are enforced by the state game or wildlife commissions. In most instances, the various states follow a classification system similar to that of the federal Endangered Species Act. Animals in imminent danger of extinction within the state are classified as "endangered species," while animals which are severely declining and could be in danger shortly are listed as "threatened species." In most states, the collection, sale or possession of any endangered species is illegal. The collection and sale of any threatened species is illegal without a permit, and possession of any threatened species is illegal unless it was obtained legally.

*Snapping turtles
are completely
banned in
California.*

Since the species is only considered within the state's borders, it is entirely possible that any particular species can be listed as endangered in one state, and only listed as threatened or perhaps not even listed at all in another. The Ornate box turtle, for example, is a common and widespread species that often appears on dealer lists. In Arkansas, however, this turtle is listed as threatened and is legally protected.

It would be impossible to list all of the various state laws regulating the possession and capture of turtles. Investigate the specific regulations that your state has for keeping turtles.

chapter 9

Conservation
of Turtles

In the United States to-
day, over a dozen turtles
are listed by the federal
government as threat-
ened or endangered,
and several dozen more
have become threatened
in the various states.
Worldwide, many turtles,
including every single
member of the large and
varied family of sea tur-

Indian Tent Turtle

tles, are considered threatened or endangered in the wild and are
vulnerable to extinction. Unfortunately, and to our everlasting
shame, nearly all of these species have become endangered through
the actions of humans. These actions range from the unintentional
but foreseeable (such as draining, cutting down and developing the
habitats upon which turtles depend) to the deliberate and malicious
(such as the harvesting of sea turtles, which pointlessly kills large
numbers every year).

Turtles in
Our World

For the most part, the major conservation groups have not demonstrated any particular interest in endangered or threatened reptiles. (One notable exception has been the efforts of the World Wildlife Fund to protect the endangered sea turtles.) Fortunately, though, there are people fighting to preserve our turtle and reptile biodiversity, along with the rest of our endangered ecosystems. And, since the pet trade has traditionally been a primary offender in driving many species to the brink of extinction, it seems only fitting that today's responsible pet owners and turtle keepers have important roles to play in herp conservation. Therefore, I would like to close this book with a description of what you, as a responsible turtle keeper, can do to help to preserve and protect these animals.

This Texas tortoise looks at home in its natural habitat surrounded by cactus plants—it is up to us to help turtles thrive in the environment that is best for them.

Herpetological Societies

The bulk of all herpetological education and conservation work in the United States is done, either directly or indirectly, by national, state and local herpetological societies. These are nonprofit bodies formed by groups of private citizens for the express purpose of furthering public education about reptiles and amphibians and promoting the conservation of wild herps. Herpetological societies also act to promote responsible keeping and captive breeding of turtles and other reptiles and amphibians.

RESEARCH ASSISTANCE

To help them meet these goals, herpetological societies carry out a number of tasks. Many herp societies carry out annual field surveys in which volunteer teams will comb wildlife habitats to take a census of the local reptile and amphibian populations. This allows researchers to study population trends of various species, and provides advance warning if populations of certain species are beginning to drop. It also helps state and federal officials monitor the populations of animals listed as threatened or endangered.

CONSERVATION EFFORTS

Most herp societies will also work with national conservation groups, such as The Nature Conservancy. These groups raise

The unusual carapace of this Pancake tortoise is a unique feature that we can appreciate due to the dedication of those who have helped protect this species.

money for the purchase of reptile and amphibian habitats, to maintain them in a natural state and insure that they will not be destroyed by future development. A few of the larger herp societies may even own and maintain reptile reserves. (Special mention should be made here of the Mid Atlantic Reptile Show, held annually in Baltimore, Maryland. All of the proceeds from this show go directly towards purchasing habitat in Costa Rica for turtles and other wildlife, and some eight hundred acres of rain forest have already been secured.)

It is inspiring to see the many herp enthusiasts gathered at this International Reptile Breeders Exposition held in Orlando, Florida.

PET SHOP MONITORING

Herp society members also monitor local pet shops, insuring that any reptiles and amphibians offered for sale are being kept in adequate conditions.

111

PUBLIC EDUCATION

The most visible work of herpetological societies, however, is in the area of public education. Most herp societies sponsor talks and shows for the public where reptiles and amphibians are exhibited and people are educated about the vital roles that reptiles play in

various ecosystems. Speakers are usually made available for school classrooms, Boy Scout troops and other groups or organizations that are interested in reptile and wildlife conservation. State and local herpetological societies may also provide witnesses and information for lawmakers who are considering regulations affecting reptiles and their keepers.

ADOPTION SERVICES

Herpetological societies also work hard to insure that all reptiles that are kept in captivity are done so

This turtle breeder is uncovering Redfoot eggs with great care.

safely, responsibly and in a way that does not endanger any wild populations. Through newsletters, meetings, guest lecturers and other methods, herp societies disseminate a large amount of information and advice concerning the captive care and breeding of a wide variety of turtles and other reptiles and amphibians. Many local herp societies also work closely with local veterinarians and run adoption services that provide good homes to herps that have been abandoned, confiscated or seized by local law enforcement or humane society officials, or simply given up for adoption.

MEMBERSHIP

I cannot encourage you strongly enough to join your local herpetological society. Although membership in a herpetological society can cost between $15 and $35 per year, it is an investment that is well worth making for any turtle enthusiast or hobbyist. Not only do you gain access to a rich source of experience and advice, but you will be helping to play an important role in maintaining and protecting these fascinating and unique creatures.

Here a keeper nets turtles from Reelfoot Lake, Tennessee, in order to protect the turtles from wrongful catching.

GIVING TALKS AND LECTURES

If there are no local herpetological societies in your area, do not despair. Your area still contains at least one usable resource that can help educate the public about the ecological roles played by reptiles and the importance of protecting them. That resource is you.

Probably the most important factor in protecting and preserving reptiles (including turtles) is public education. Although few people have the irrational fear of turtles that they have of snakes or spiders, most people have at best only a vague understanding of these animals and their needs, and most of what they do understand is usually inaccurate.

With respect from humans, this Galapagos tortoise will have the chance to live longer than you and even your children.

This sort of public education is probably the most important work that any turtle hobbyist can do. If you are comfortable with public speaking, use your skills to talk to as many people as you can. Go to grade school classrooms, Bible school classes, Boy Scout

113

troops or local environmental associations. If you don't know the scientific names of your pets, or can't identify all of the turtles that are native to Latin America, or can't tell a quadrate bone from a tibia,

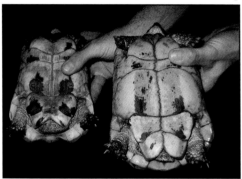

that's okay. As long as you have an understanding of what ecosystems are and how they work, and what roles turtles play in them (and I hope this book has helped you in that understanding), you know all the stuff that is important. Beyond that, it is merely a matter of exposing people to the animals, allowing them to see for themselves the unique behavior patterns and the dazzling array of colors that make turtles so fascinating. The animals themselves are their own best advertisement.

Here an instructor is demonstrating how to differentiate the sex of Egyptian Greek tortoises.

Captive Breeding

One of the most concrete contributions that turtle keepers can make to reptile conservation is a vigorous and steady program of captive breeding.

There are two different but important possible goals for a captive breeding program. The first is captive breeding of endangered and threatened reptiles for the ultimate purpose of reintroducing them back into the wild. The major difficulty faced by such programs, of course, is the continuing destruction of habitats, which too often means that there is no longer any "wild" left for the animals to be released into.

Only a few turtles have been the object of intensive captive breeding attempts. The seven species of sea turtles (all of which are threatened or endangered) have been the target of a program that enables volunteers to monitor known breeding areas and remove the eggs shortly after laying. The eggs are then artificially incubated and hatched, and the young turtles released to the wild. On the Galapagos Islands, the Darwin Memorial Research Station has been breeding the islands' giant tortoises. Four of the Galapagos subspecies, however, are already extinct, and two others are effectively extinct since they consist only of aged individuals past breeding age.

The second goal of captive breeding, however, is very much within the scope of the amateur breeder and local herpetological societies. One of the chief threats facing many wild populations of turtles, both within the United States and abroad,

With Supervision, this Eatern box turtle and a cat can peacefully coexist in nature.

is overcollection for the pet trade. Several million live reptiles are imported into the US each year, nearly all of them wild-caught, and most of them as pets. Between 1967 and 1971, for instance, over one million Spur Thigh tortoises were exported just from Morocco to Britain, while Yugoslavia exported over 400,000 Greek tortoises in 1971 alone. Few wild populations can withstand that sort of drain for very long.

One partial solution to this problem is to encourage captive breeding of these species, so they can be made available to hobbyists and collectors without the necessity of taking any more animals from the wild. Unfortunately, turtles are not as widely bred as are the more popular lizards or snakes, and captive-bred turtles are a rarity in the pet trade. For this reason, responsible captive breeding of these species is to be actively encouraged and supported.

Of course, many of the most endangered species are difficult to breed because we simply do not know enough about their biology and habits to duplicate them in captivity. It therefore becomes a priority for serious hobbyists to identify the conditions under which these turtles can be kept and breeding induced. Such knowledge will be vital to protecting and maintaining these species—and serious amateurs are fully capable of discovering and providing such knowledge.

For that reason, I strongly encourage every turtle keeper and hobbyist who has been inspired by this book to gain a level of experience and confidence that will allow you to undertake your own captive-breeding research. Start with those species that breed fairly easily but are not commonly bred—box turtles and Painted turtles would be good choices. From there, go on to the more difficult and rare species. For many, effective breeding in captivity may be all that stands between the species and extinction.

LOOK BEYOND YOUR BACKYARD:

Educate children to respect endangered animals

Keep your turtle free of *Salmonella*

Share your resources with new turtle owners

Make a commitment to be a responsible turtle keeper

Beyond
the
Basics

chapter 10

Resources

Further Reading

BOOKS

Behler, John, and F. Wayne King. *The Audubon Society Field Guide to North American Reptiles and Amphibians,* Alfred A. Knopf, New York, NY, 1979.

Carr, Archie. *The Reptiles,* Life Nature Library, Time Inc., New York, NY, 1963.

Conant, Roger. *A Field Guide to Reptiles and Amphibians of Eastern and Central North America,* Houghton Mifflin Co., Boston, MA, 1975.

Mattison, Chris. *The Care of Reptiles and Amphibians in Captivity,* Blandford, London, England, 1992.

Obst, Fritz Jurgen. *Turtles, Tortoises and Terrapins,* St. Martin's Press, New York, NY, 1986.

Rosenfeld, Arthur. *Exotic Pets,* Simon and Schuster, Inc., New York, NY, 1987.

Stebbins, R.C. *A Field Guide to Western Reptiles and Amphibians,* Houghton Mifflin Co., Boston, MA, 1966.

Vogel, Zdenek. *Reptiles and Amphibians; Their Care and Behavior,* Studio Vista, London, England, 1964.

MAGAZINES

Amateur Herpetoculturalist
Wahsatch Alliance of Herpetoculturalists
c/o TAH
PO Box 1907
Casper, WY 82602

Captive Breeding
PO Box 87100
Canton, MI 48187

Reptile and Amphibian Magazine
RD #3 Box 3709-A
Pottsville, PA 17901

Reptiles Magazine
Subscription Dept.
PO Box 6040
Mission Viejo, CA 92690

Breeders and Turtle Dealers

Central Florida Reptile Farm
4800 Kumquat St.
Cocoa, FL 32926

Glades Herp
PO Box 50911
Fort Meyers, FL 33905

Harford Reptile Breeding Center
Al Zulich
PO Box 914
Bel Air, MD 21014-0914

International Reptile Supply
6681 62nd Ave. N
Pinellas Park, FL 34665

Reptile Enterprises Inc.
PO Box 1145
Bushnell, FL 33513

Special Care Pet Center
5 W. Prospect Ave.
Pittsburgh, PA 15205

VJ's Exotic Reptiles
10 Avenue O (on W. 11th St.)
Brooklyn, NY 11204

National Herpetological Societies and Associations

American Federation of Herpetoculturalists
PO Box 3000670
Escondido, CA 92030-0067
(Publishes *The Vivarium.*)

American Society of Icthyologists and Herpetologists
Business Office
PO Box 1897
Lawrence, KS 66044-8897
(Publishes the quarterly journal *Copeia.*)

Endangered Turtle Protection Foundation
PO Box 4617
Greenville, DE 19807

National Herpetological Alliance
PO Box 5143
Chicago, IL 60680-5143

Society for the Study of Reptiles and Amphibians
Karen Toepfer
PO Box 626
Hays, KS 67601-0626

Local Herpetological Societies

This listing is far from complete. If you contact the societies listed below, they may be able to point you to a local herp society that is closer to you.

Fairbanks Herpetocultural Society
Taryn Merdes
PO Box 71309
Fairbanks, AK 99707

Arizona Herpetological Association
PO Box 39127
Phoenix, AZ 85069-9127

Arkansas Herpetological Association
Glyn Turnipseed
418 N. Fairbanks
Russelville, AR 72801

Northern California Herpetological Society
PO Box 1363
Davis, CA 95616-1363

San Diego Turtle and Tortoise Society
13963 Lyons Valley Rd.
Jamul, CA 92035

California Turtle and Tortoise Society
Westchester Chapter
PO Box 90252
Los Angeles, CA 90009

California Turtle and Tortoise Society
Foothill Chapter
PO Box 51002
Pasadena, CA 91115-1002

Sacramento Turtle and Tortoise Club
Felice Rood
25 Starlit Circle
Sacramento, CA 95831

Southern California Herpetology Association
PO Box 2932
Santa Fe Springs, CA 90607

Colorado Herpetological Society
PO Box 15381
Denver, CO 80215

Southern New England Herpetological Association
470 Durham Rd.
Madison, CT 06443-2060

Delaware Herpetological Society
Ashland Nature Center
Brackenville and Barley Mill Rds.
Hockessin, DE 19707

Gopher Tortoise Council
Patricia Ashton
611 NW 79th Dr.
Gainesville, FL 32607

Beyond the
Basics

West Florida Herpetological Society
3055 Panama Rd.
Pensacola, FL 32526

Turtle and Tortoise Club of Florida
Ed Hughes
PO Box 239
Sanford, FL 32772-0239

Central Florida Herpetological Society
PO Box 3277
Winter Haven, FL 33881

Georgia Herpetological Society
Department of Herpetology, Atlanta Zoo
800 Cherokee Ave. SE
Atlanta, GA 30315

Idaho Herpetological Society
PO Box 6329
Boise, ID 83707

Central Illinois Herpetological Society
1125 W. Lake Ave.
Peoria, IL 61614

Hoosier Herpetological Society
PO Box 40544
Indianapolis, IN 46204

Iowa Herpetological Society
PO Box 166
Norwalk, IA 50211

Kansas Herpetological Society
Museum of Natural History, Dyche Hall
University of Kansas
Lawrence, KS 66045

Central Kentucky Herpetological Society
PO Box 12227
Lexington, KY 40581-2227

Louisiana Herpetological Society
Museum of Natural History
Foster Hall, LSU
Baton Rouge, LA 70803

Maryland Herpetological Society
Natural History Society
2643 N. Charles St.
Baltimore, MD 21218

New England Herpetological Society
PO Box 1082
Boston, MA 02103

Michigan Society of Herpetologists
321 W. Oakland
Lansing, MI 48906

Minnesota Herpetological Society
Bell Museum of Natural History
10 Church St. SE
Minneapolis, MN 55455-0104

Southern Mississippi Herpetological Society
PO Box 1685
Ocean Springs, MS 39564

St. Louis Herpetological Society
Harry Steinmann
PO Box 220153
Kirkwood, MO 63122

Tortoise Group
5157 Poncho Circle
Las Vegas, NV 89119

Northern Nevada Herpetological Society
Don Bloomer
PO Box 21282
Reno, NV 89502-1282

New York Turtle and Tortoise Society
PO Box 878
Orange, NJ 07051-0878

**Association for the Conservation of
   Turtles and Tortoises**
RD 4, Box 368
Sussex, NJ 07461

New Mexico Herpetological Society
University of New Mexico
Department of Biology
Albuquerque, NM 87131

New York Herpetological Society
PO Box 1245
Grand Central Station
New York, NY 10163-1245

North Carolina Herpetological Society
State Museum
PO Box 29555
Raleigh, NC 27626

Northern Ohio Association of Herpetologists
Department of Biology
Case Western Reserve University
Cleveland, OH 44106

Central Ohio Herpetological Society
217 E. New England Ave.
Worthington, OH 43085

Oklahoma Herpetological Society
Oklahoma City Chapter
Oklahoma Zoo
2101 NE 50th
Oklahoma City, OK 73111

Oklahoma Herpetological Society
Tulsa Chapter
5701 E. 36th St. N
Tulsa, OK 74115

Oregon Herpetological Society
WISTEC
PO Box 1518
Eugene, OR 97440

Lehigh Valley Herpetological Society
Rich Rosevear
PO Box 9171
Allentown, PA 18105-9171

Philadelphia Herpetological Society
Mark Miller
PO Box 52261
Philadelphia, PA 19115

Philadelphia Turtle and Tortoise Club
Mark Miller
9573 Walley Ave.
Philadelphia, PA 19115

Pittsburgh Herpetological Society
Pittsburgh Zoo
1 Hill Rd.
Pittsburgh, PA 15206

Rhode Island Herpetological Association
30 Metropolitan Rd.
Providence, RI 02909

South Carolina Herpetological Society
James L. Knight
PO Box 100107
Columbia, SC 29230

Turtle and Tortoise Society of Charleston
121 Hamlet Rd.
Summerville, SC 29485

Houston Turtle and Tortoise Society
PO Box 1528
Friendswood, TX 77456-1528

Lubbock Turtle and Tortoise Society
Joe Cain
5708 64th St.
Lubbock, TX 79424

Texas Herpetological Society
Hutchinson Hall of Science
31st at Canton
Lubbock, TX 79410

Utah Herpetological Society
Hogle Zoo
PO Box 8475
Salt Lake City, UT 84108

Washington Herpetological Society
12420 Rock Ridge Rd.
Herndon, VA 22070

Pacific Northwest Herpetological Society
PO Box 70231
Bellevue, WA 98008

Wisconsin Herpetological Society
PO Box 366
Germantown, WI 53022